a Place Called Home

a spirituality for anxious times

HARRIET CROSBY

THOMAS NELSON PUBLISHERS

Nashville • Atlanta • London • Vancouver

Printed in the United States of America

Published in Nashville, Tennessee, by Thomas Nelson, Inc., Publishers, and distributed in Canada by Word Communications, Ltd., Richmond, British Columbia.

The Bible version used in this publication is the NEW REVISED STANDARD VERSION. Copyright © 1989 by the Division of Christian Education of the National Council of the Churches of Christ in the U.S.A. All rights reserved.

Library of Congress Cataloging-in-Publication Data

Crosby, Harriet.
    A place called home : a spirituality for anxious times / Harriet E. Crosby.
        p.   cm.
    ISBN 0-7852-7607-6
    1. Home—Religious aspects—Christianity. 2. Spiritual life—Christianity. 3. Crosby, Harriet. I. Title.
BV4501.2.C7517 1996
248.4—dc20   96–33356
                                                                    CIP

Printed in the United States of America.

1 2 3 4 5 6 — 02 01 00 99 98 97

For Mom and Dad

I couldn't have done it without you.
Here's to the townhouse.

CONTENTS

ACKNOWLEDGMENTS

Many thanks to
Lonnie Hull DuPont,
a constant source of personal
and editorial inspiration.

the Foundation:
An Invitation

Numb from head to toe, I signed each paper that was placed before me. Friends had warned me what an awful experience signing the mortgage on your first home can be. They were right.

The search for a home of my very own was finally over. Suddenly, I was a homeowner. A *homeowner*. At long last. I was surprised that I didn't feel happier. Instead, I felt shocked and overwhelmed by the enormous responsibility—and debt—I had assumed. I felt like someone had just shot my dog.

I had worked fifteen years to save up, all by myself, for a down payment on a home. Despite a prolonged recession, the San Francisco Bay Area, where I live, is still the most expensive place in the United States to buy a home. During the months of searching for an affordable home, I was constantly aware that my life's savings were at stake. I worried myself sick over whether, at forty years old, I ought to jump into a soft housing market with no guarantee of a return on my investment. I also worried endlessly about neighborhoods (I could only afford to live in "emerging neighborhoods" where crime is a reality), about termites (most houses in my price range came with a $10,000 infestation), about mortgage rates (which were rapidly rising), and about getting fired from my job (I work for a big bank notorious for lay-offs).

After signing all the papers, my realtor unceremoniously dropped me off in front of my new, sixty-seven-year-old home, handed me the key, and waved good-bye. I stood on the porch, overwhelmed again by the life-changing decision I had just made. I inserted the key in the lock. My mind told me I had made the right decision. Friends had repeatedly affirmed my reasons for buying a home and this house in particular. But my anxiety about becoming a homeowner persisted. Did I do the right thing? What about crime in this neighborhood? If I lose my job tomorrow, who will pay the mortgage? I just couldn't turn off all the anxiety that had developed during the months of house searching. On and on a litany of worry swirled repeatedly in my head, dulling my joy upon first entering my very own front door.

That's what makes anxiety so debilitating—it eats away at joy in our lives. Prolonged worry over someone or something requires a great deal of emotional energy. A friend once described anxious feelings as being constantly vigilant—always waiting and watching for something awful to happen.

Underneath constant worry is always the expectation that something bad is about to happen. After all, whoever worried about something *good* just around the corner? Anxiety projects our emotional life into a future that in some way threatens us or someone we love. And worry is habit-forming. It can become so focused on the future, so all-consuming that there is no energy left over to fully experience positive feelings of joy, love, or even simple contentment in the present. The joy I should have experienced signing the papers that made me a homeowner, the joy I should have known when I first walked through my front door, had been eaten away by anxiety.

Inspecting the Foundation

Before buying my house, I had it thoroughly inspected. I told myself that if the inspector found anything wrong with the foundation, the deal would be off. After an exhaustive four-hour examination of the house from top to bottom, the inspector said of the foundation, "This house has good bones. And that's unusual in older starter homes around here. It's well-built and has been well-maintained over the years." I was thrilled—and terrified. "That's great!" I replied. But inside I was thinking, *Uh-oh. I guess this is a sign that I should actually buy the house and stop dreaming about it.* It was my first twinge of "buyer's remorse," my first baby step onto anxiety's treadmill.

"Why do you call me 'Lord, Lord,' and do not do what I tell you? I will show you what someone is like who comes to me, hears my words, and acts on them. That one is like a man building a house, who dug deeply and laid the foundation on rock; when a flood arose, the river burst against that house but could not shake it, because it had been well built. But the one who hears and does not act is like a man who built a house on the ground without a foundation. When the river burst against it, immediately it fell, and great was the ruin of that house."   Luke 6:46–49

Jesus is interested in foundations, those blocks on which we build our houses, our lives. He tells his disciples of two home builders. The first builder I like to call Sam. Sam took the time and trouble to dig and work hard until he hit rock on which to lay his foundation. After his home was built, the river flooded but the house remained secure. On the other hand, Bob, the second home builder, couldn't be bothered to dig. He just built his house on topsoil, which washed away with his house during the flood. I've always imagined that Sam and Bob built the exact same house. Whether the house stood or fell depended on the condition of the foundation.

Anxiety is like an infestation of termites. Invisibly it eats away at our foundation until nothing is left to support us. I must confess that I was not prepared for buyer's remorse, in spite of being warned repeatedly by friends. The whole experience and the anxiety it produced showed me that, while my new home's foundation was in great shape, the foundation on which I'd built my *spiritual* house was on sinking sand. It wasn't until I was absolutely overwhelmed by anxiety that I thought of inspecting my spiritual foundation.

A Place Called Home is a call for an inspection. We examine our lives—especially during anxiety-filled times—in order to hear Jesus' words once again and obey them. And that means discovering the infestation, the source of the anxiety. Reflecting on the words of Jesus, each chapter represents a room in my house. Each room offers a different way of letting go of our need to anxiously control the uncontrollable by living and relaxing in Christ, our true home. As we walk through my house, we will explore different expressions of faith, including hospitality, prayer, simplicity, and gratitude—all of which help us in our struggle with anxiety to make our home with Jesus.

Our foundation, of course, is constructed on the words of Jesus. During anxious times we need to hear, I mean *really hear*, Jesus' words again. His words were like a life raft to me as I was going down for the third time under a flood of anxiety. I found this constant stream of anxiety to be very "noisy." The worry chattered ceaselessly as I played various scenarios of "horribleness" at top volume. I couldn't hear a thing—least of all the gentle whisper of Christ. Of course, it became clear to me that I was not living simply, but instead doing everything I could to complicate my life and drown out hearing God call my name.

We live in an age of anxiety. As we approach the end of the twentieth century, many feel a leveling off or even decline in the standard of living in this country. Everything from rising crime rates to a constantly shifting economy to an increasingly angry political climate has left many feeling nervous and uneasy. We are worried about the future for ourselves, our children, and our communities.

In addition to a general sense of unease, most of us are occasionally anxious for various personal reasons. For example, we occasionally experience acute anxiety during major life transitions, such as getting married, changing careers, or buying a first home. Although positive, such transitions can trigger plenty of anxious feelings that may surprise us. After all, we tell ourselves, we're sitting on top of the world, so what is there to worry about?

Some major life transitions result from experiencing a significant loss, such as the death of a loved one, the loss of a job, or the failing of health. During such times anxious feelings are not surprising. But our anxiety is often intensified by simultaneous feelings of grief and deep sadness.

Still, others of us can't remember a time when we weren't worrying about someone or something. Our anxiety is chronic. I was born anxious. My mother tells the story of watching me as a baby in my crib as I repeatedly twisted a bit of baby hair around my finger and pulled it out by the roots.

I still have a small bald spot on the left side of my head. As I look back on my childhood, teenage years, and subsequent adulthood, I have come to realize that I worry neurotically over situations and people beyond my control.

Whether our anxiety is focused on our society or a time in our personal lives, whether it is acute or chronic, not having control over someone or something is what we all share at the root of our anxious feelings. If we rationally examine the source of our worry, we can see that either our own decision to do something sets in motion forces we no longer control—or circumstances already beyond our control threaten our lives in some way. For example, a friend of mine has built a career at a corporation which has become famous in recent months for downsizing. Corporate circumstances beyond her control threaten her career and it worries her. In my own situation, I made a good, carefully reasoned decision to buy a house. That choice meant I no longer had control over the safety of the neighborhood or the rising mortgage rates. But just knowing I had no control didn't stop me from worrying anyway.

Acute or chronic anxiety results from the persistent, misguided belief that we can somehow control the things that cause us to worry. We subtly tell ourselves that all we have to do is figure out how to be better people or how to pray harder or how to regain control we never really had and all of our worries will disappear. The best remedy for such wrong-headed belief is faith.

Christian faith is the living out of only one belief—the reality of God in Jesus Christ through the Holy Spirit. Believing that God came to the world in Jesus Christ, who continues to work in the world through the Holy Spirit, means living a life of faith. Having faith is acting on that belief with our heads, our hearts, our bodies, and our spirits. Faith is trusting with our whole being in the love, grace, and mercy of God given to each of us in Jesus Christ. Being faithful means continually sacrificing the belief that we have ultimate control over our lives, the lives of those we love, and our communities, and trusting that God is at work in spite of what we see, in spite of what we believe about our world, and in spite of how worried and anxious we are.

The process of buying a house helped me see that my need for a "dream home" was really an expression of a deeper spiritual longing to be "home" with Jesus. My idea of a dream home was always a part of my decision to buy a house. I've never really experienced my dream home; none of several houses throughout my childhood or the subsequent apartments I lived in as an adult came close to being my dream home.

So when I began the search to buy my first house, I kept looking for my dream home. I set out in quest of an English Tudor style house with three bedrooms, two full baths, a gourmet kitchen, a light-filled breakfast room with a bow window, a formal dining room with a built-in breakfront, a large English garden, a detached studio with French doors, a laundry room, and a two-car garage—all in a fashionable, quiet neighborhood with lots of trees. By the time I'd looked at the tenth house in my price range, I realized my dream home would *remain* a dream. I began to wonder, besides just wanting to buy a physical dwelling that would cost half a million dollars in the Bay Area, what was really so emotionally powerful about my dream home? What did "home" really mean?

For me, a dream home has always been a place where I can be completely relaxed and free of care. It is a place that is safe, a place where I feel absolutely secure. Home is inviting, warm, and welcoming to all, a place filled with laughter and love. Home is forgiving, a place where I can be most fully myself, the person God created me to be. Home is where my heart is.

I began to see that my dream home is not an earthly home. A million dollar house does not make a home. I began to understand that my true dream home is my Father's house. It is wherever Jesus lives.

> *"Do not let your hearts be troubled. Believe in God, believe also in me. In my Father's house there are many dwelling places. If it were not so, would I have told you that I go to prepare a place for you? And if I go and prepare a place for, I will come again and will take you to myself, so that where I am, there you may be also."*
> John 14:1–3

These words of Jesus are among the most comforting in all Scripture. Jesus looks directly into our hearts and sees that we are troubled, worried, and anxious. "You believe in God," he says, "believe also in me." Subtly, Jesus tells us not to believe in the anxiety we harbor in our hearts; he directs our focus away from our hearts' trouble to our hearts' home. Notice that Jesus doesn't tell us to get a grip on ourselves, to stop worrying, and to get control of whatever is troubling us. He doesn't even tell us to think positively or pray harder. Jesus isn't into spiritual self-help. Neither does he dismiss our troubles as silly or even sinful. Instead, Jesus welcomes our troubled and anxious hearts into the Father's house, a house with many rooms. And one of those rooms has our name on it. We are to come home to live with Jesus.

The best remedy for anxiety is living with Jesus every day. Jesus opens wide the door of his Father's house to welcome us home, troubled hearts and all. For the grace of God is greater than all of our worst worries; the love of God bears all of our worst imaginings; the mercy of God is deeper than our worst fears. Jesus makes his home with us, and any house, no matter how humble or how grand, is home when we open our hearts to the presence of Christ.

Reading *A Place Called Home* won't make worries magically disappear. But then we don't live our lives by magic; we live our lives by faith in Jesus Christ, who touches our troubled hearts and calls us home. Come with me now and make yourself at home.

CHAPTER I

the Living Room:
Simplicity

*Just then a lawyer stood up to test Jesus. "Teacher,"
he said, "what must I do to inherit eternal life?" He
said to him, "What is written in the law? What do you
read there?" He answered, "You shall love the Lord
your God with all your heart, and with all your soul,
and with all your strength, and with all your mind;
and your neighbor as yourself." And he said to him,
"You have given the right answer; do this, and you will
live."* Luke 10:25–28

Not long after I bought my house, I met my newly-married friend Suzanne for lunch in a San Francisco café. As we sat down to eat, I asked her how married life was treating her. Suzanne replied she hadn't been doing very well, but couldn't understand why. "I love Don so much," she told me. "He's sensitive and kind and so much fun to be with. And he loves me dearly. But I'm so anxious all the time. I always feel like something terrible is about to happen."

The year before, Suzanne fell in love with Don, her best friend. Well into her forties, Suzanne had already accepted the possibility she might not marry. So getting married was like a dream come true for her. But she couldn't rid herself of a crippling anxiety. She convinced herself that every time Don left the house she would get a phone call telling her of his death. Whether he was on his way to work or running an errand, each time Don left the house Suzanne told him to be careful. She told him of her fear and he had been very understanding and sympathetic. But Suzanne's anxiety remained high.

By the time we met for lunch a year later, Suzanne was miserable. She knew the source of her anxiety. She told me that many years ago she had been engaged to a wonderful man who died suddenly. No matter how often she told herself "that was the past," she couldn't help feeling that the same fate awaited Don. When he left the house, Suzanne compulsively imagined all kinds of horrible scenarios involving Don's demise and how she might prevent them. In short, Suzanne's anxiety was eating away at the joy in her marriage.

Anxiety complicates our lives. As if we don't have enough to do already, anxiety turns us into full-time vigilantes. Like Suzanne, we hunt for real or imagined threats to ourselves or those we love. Fueled by fear, anxiety builds as we worry over ways to prevent something bad from happening. We spin endless scenarios in which we are able to maintain or get control of anxious situations. Anxiety puts us on a hopeless treadmill of fear and worry that brings no relief.

I'm not telling you anything you don't already know. If you're like me, you've told yourself a million times to relax, that worry doesn't change anything or anybody. And if you haven't told yourself to relax and quit worrying, I'll bet many well-meaning friends and family members have. Yet worries continue to abound and anxiety builds, sometimes to the proverbial "fever pitch." But there is a better way to live, a way that can ease us off that anxious treadmill. It is life in Jesus Christ.

In Luke, chapter 10, Jesus rejoices in the Holy Spirit, thanking the Father "because you have hidden these things from the wise and the intelligent and have revealed them to infants; . . ." (Luke 10:21). He then turns to his disciples, "infants," the so-called simpletons in the faith and in the world, and calls them "blessed." But a member of the local intelligencia, a lawyer, overheard Jesus' crack about the "wise and intelligent." We can almost see the wheels turning in the lawyer's mind. He wants to prove to Jesus that only the wise and intelligent can possibly understand great spiritual truths that grant access to eternal life. And so he stands up to "test" Jesus—"What must I do to inherit eternal life?" Underneath the bravado, however, is a sincere, heartfelt question—*What must I do to live?* The lawyer thinks Jesus will propose a complicated set of laws and regulations that only he, an experienced lawyer, can follow. Instead, Jesus tests the lawyer's knowledge of the law. "What is written in the law? What do you read there?" *But that's simple,* the lawyer thinks to himself, and answers, "To love the Lord your God . . . and your neighbor as yourself." "Do this," says Jesus, "and you will live."

The secret of living is the same secret to eternal life. Little children know it; even simpletons know it. The secret is simplicity itself—*love*. Love the Lord your God with all your heart, soul, strength, and mind, and your neighbor as yourself. That's all there is to it.

Anxiety feeds on life's complications, on striving to meet expectations, on perfectly following rules and regulations, on meeting deadlines, on doing more and more and more and more. But to live, to really *live*, in Christ requires only one thing—to love with abandon and no thought for tomorrow; to love regardless of whatever anxious times we may be living through; to love as though our lives depended on it.

I like my living room. I spend a lot of time there doing nothing in particular. When I'm in my living room, I just *live*. Right after I moved in, I painted the room's original dingy-beige walls a very soft, pale yellow; the vaulted ceiling is pure white, as is the art deco molding around each window. The room is a perpetual springtime. A bright floral-print couch, decorated in blues, pinks, reds, greens, and yellows, sits against one wall. Above the couch hangs a long, framed print of a 1948 oil painting called *Spring Party*, by Janet Fish. In the corner opposite and to one side of the bay window is an oversized easy chair and ottoman, slipcovered in dark green ticking stripe. On the other side of the window is a pine armoire, which hides a television and stereo. The fire place, built into the furthest wall from the entry, is surrounded by two long casement windows. The dark hardwood floors are accented by white area rugs. Sunlight pours through the windows each morning.

My living room is a simple, welcoming room. It's simplicity suits me—there I can relax and enjoy the sunlight. As in many homes, my living room is the first room guests see upon entering the house and that's important because it is a reflection of how I live. It is a place that soothes anxious feelings. (By now I think I've made it reasonably clear that I am a naturally, chronically anxious person, if not a raging neurotic!) Anxious people like myself don't need any more stimulation than is absolutely necessary—we're already worried to death about something or someone without added external stimuli.

Simplicity is not just another interior design option. It is also one of the great expressions of Christian faith. Simplicity is devoting our lives to one thing and one thing only—to *loving* the Lord our God with our whole being and our neighbors as ourselves.

Simplicity is the great enemy of anxiety. Just as anxiety complicates life, practicing living the simple life is an attempt to uncomplicate life. To live the "simple life" does not mean living the "easy life". Simple living often requires hard work. To offer a somewhat dramatic example: People in recovery from addictions are, in reality, simplifying their lives on a daily basis. These folk know that their recovery and healing means trusting in the power of God every moment of every day. Being in recovery isn't easy, but it is liberating. Recovering addicts and alcoholics know that living sober is the liberating experience of giving up control, of "letting go and letting God." Giving up control of the universe to God liberates us to love God and neighbor every day.

Annie Dillard once wrote that "anyone who thinks he is in control is asleep at the switch."[1] The art of living the simple life under the lordship of Christ is letting go of the anxious need to control whatever is uncontrollable in our lives.

In C. S. Lewis's children's book, *The Lion, the Witch, and the Wardrobe*, Lucy says of Aslan, the lion and Christ figure in the story, "He isn't safe; but he is good."[2] When we trust our worries, ourselves, and our loved ones to the living God of the universe, we give up control. We let God have his way over uncontrollable situations and people. The outcome is not ours to produce but God's to direct. A particular outcome may or may not be what we want. God is not safe. But God is good. And in God's goodness can we live and relax.

But let's go back to Suzanne. As she and I continued to talk over lunch, I found I was having startlingly similar feelings as hers. I realized Suzanne and I were sharing the same experience in spite of the fact that I've never been married and Suzanne has never owned a home. We were both living in a state of high anxiety. Ever since I had bought my house I had become a vigilante regarding crime in the neighborhood. I worried constantly—and I mean *constantly*—about someone burglarizing my little house or breaking in to attack me in the middle of the night.

Expecting the worst, I installed security doors and a burglar alarm system, sealed the door to the downstairs basement, put a grille over the basement window, and installed floodlights over the garage and in the backyard. Then I sat in my house like a prisoner on death row, waiting for the worst to happen. To say that I was anxious is an understatement. I was wild. Such anxiety did *not* help me love God or my neighbors any better. Paralyzed by fear verging on paranoia, I wasn't living anymore.

The more Suzanne and I talked, the more I understood the anxiety we shared. Both of us had set sail onto uncharted waters: Suzanne was white-water rafting her way through a new marriage; I was dog paddling on a sea of buyer's remorse. To put it less metaphorically, we were both plodding through anxious times, major life transitions that were completely new to us and outside our previous experiences.

Although Suzanne's new marriage and my new house were *good* things, they were *new* experiences and, as a result, left two confident, successful women reduced to quivering masses of anxious insecurity. Each of us had left the familiar, safe harbors of landlords and singleness to sail a sea of discovery. Now landlords and the single life may have had some serious drawbacks, but at least they were *known* drawbacks and, therefore, safe. Suzanne and I no longer felt that safety. In our own ways, each of us cast a longing eye back on old days when we felt we had life under some kind of control.

During my lunch with Suzanne I discovered something else we had in common. For both of us, our dreams had come true—Suzanne married a good man who loves her, I bought my first home. Suzanne and I found that while our dreams remained in our hearts, we could control them. When my dream house was still a dream, I could control what it would be like with my imagination. I would daydream about the size of the living room or the kind of windows it would contain. I would imagine a gazebo in the middle of the flower garden in back. With my mind's eye I would look up and down the quiet, tree-lined street where I would one day live. Of course, my dream home existed in a world free of crime.

When my dream of owning a home became a reality, I had a *real* house to maintain, decorate, and improve. No longer did I dream about a bow window in the breakfast room or a marble mantle over the fireplace. My real house doesn't have such things, and adding these features to my house is well beyond my financial means. And my real house is located in a neighborhood where crime is definitely a reality.

When our dreams become reality, we no longer control

them. In a way, our dreams come alive and take on form and substance to live in the real world. And in the real world good and bad things happen. Now Suzanne's marriage is no longer a dream. Her husband Don is a real human being, subject to all the potential accidents and diseases that may or may not be in store for any one of us. My house is no longer a dream. It is part of the real world, subject to earthquake, fire, and flood, as well as the ebbs and flows of a changing neighborhood. I can buy insurance against such things, but I cannot control them. Both Suzanne and I have to learn to live in a world where we are not ultimately in control.

Living a simple life helps us let go of the need to be in control to love again. Simple living relieves paralyzing fear and anxiety to let Jesus be Lord so we can get on with the business of loving God and our neighbors.

A Well-Swept House

"When the unclean spirit has gone out of a person, it wanders through waterless regions looking for a resting place, but not finding any, it says, 'I will return to my house from which I came.' When it comes, it finds it swept and put in order. Then it goes and brings seven other spirits more evil than itself, and they enter and live there; and the last state of that person is worse than the first." Luke 11:24–26

Imagine for a moment that the "unclean spirit" of which Jesus spoke in Luke is anxiety. I'm not talking about occasional bouts of nervousness. No, the unclean spirit here can be a debilitating anxiety fueled by a real or imagined fear.

In my own experience with such anxiety I would thrust aside worry and fear for a little while and get a break from anxious feelings. But sooner or later the anxiety returned, bringing more worries and "vain imaginings" with it. I'd feel like the homeowner who had cleaned and ordered her house only to have seven more unclean spirits move in and wreak chaos. Again, I was trapped on anxiety's treadmill, where worries crowd 'round and life seems hopelessly complicated.

Unclean spirits, it seems, can't stand a well-swept, orderly house. Even those who build on good foundations and "hear [Jesus'] words and do them" have to clean house. Anxiety can't live in a clean and tidy house; and I can't live in the chaos and confusion anxiety creates when it takes up residence in my spiritual living room. One of us has to go.

So I have found that I need to make a periodic clean sweep of my spiritual house. Here, the discipline of simplicity and God's grace help me to bring order out of chaos, to break it down into small pieces, and sweep the pieces from my inner house.

Living simply is the art of simplifying—untangling complicated feelings and situations, sorting out what is real from what is imagined, uncovering anxiety's infestation in our spiritual foundations. As my anxiety deepened and intensified after the purchase of my home, I developed a series of simple questions to help me put my spiritual house in order:

- *What are the* facts *that cause me anxiety?* I have a lot more responsibility now. I bought a sixty-seven-year-old house that needs more fixing up than I realized. I've assumed a mortgage that takes half my monthly paycheck. The value of real estate in California is still declining. My neighborhood has a high crime rate.

- *What am I* imagining *to cause me anxiety?* That I'll be murdered in my bed. That, in a few years, I'll sell my house at a loss. That termites are eating away the foundation. That townhouses are much better buys for women living alone. That I'll never be able to afford to fix up the house the way I'd like. That everybody in the universe has a better house than I and, therefore, everybody is happier than I.

- *What are the* facts *that can help relieve my anxiety?* Despite its age, my house has been well-maintained and is in excellent condition. Not everybody in the neighborhood is being murdered in their beds. I can pay my mortgage and bills each month, with a little left over for home improvements. I don't really know where the California real estate market will be in a few years. My friends and my faith can support me as I learn to live with this new responsibility. I know nothing about townhouses.

- *What can I control regarding this situation/person?* I can make my house more secure and start a neighborhood watch program. I can refinance. I can pay for home improvements over a period of months and years, rather than do it all tomorrow. I can ask for God's help when my imagination begins to run wild and makes me nervous.

- *What is uncontrollable regarding this situation/person?* The crime rate in my neighborhood. The age of the house. The California real estate market.

- *What do I want God to do to help me with this anxiety?* To continue to provide for me and protect my neighborhood, and help me relax in Christ.

- *How is God calling me to love him and others today?* God wants me to relax in his love for me *today* so that I can do good work for my colleagues at the bank.

Notice how brief and simple the questions are. There is only one rule to practicing simplicity—*keep it simple*. I wanted to simplify and untangle the inner chaos so that I could rebuild my spiritual foundation on Christ's words. The little question-and-answer format helped me simplify, untangle, and pare down anxious feelings so that I could expose the source.

I wish I could tell you that once I answered a few simple questions, anxiety fled my spiritual house never to return. But

I continue to struggle with buyer's remorse and the resulting anxiety. It's like good housekeeping. A good housekeeper doesn't clean the house once; good housekeepers regularly clean and tidy their houses. So I regularly call for an inspection and sweep my spiritual house clean. I answer these same questions again and again to help me hear Christ's words and do them.

A Well-Maintained House

"But know this: if the owner of the house had known at what hour the thief was coming, he would not have let his house be broken into. You also must be ready, for the Son of Man is coming at an unexpected hour." Luke 12:39–40

When I bought my home, I had no idea that my Girl Scout training would come in handy. Good home maintenance can be summed up in the motto "be prepared." The roof inspector informed me that though the roof was only two years old, it had been repeatedly patched in several places, which might be a problem in the future. I wondered, *why would someone need to repeatedly patch a relatively new roof?* But I decided not to take a chance, figuring an ounce of prevention is worth a pound of cure. Immediately after buying the house in July, I put a brand-new roof on it. The following winter, California had the worst series of rain storms in the century. During one storm Oakland got five inches of rain in one day. I was prepared. My new roof held up beautifully, though the garage flooded three times.

Any home owner knows keeping the house well-maintained isn't much fun. I don't know anyone who enjoys fixing the plumbing or replacing a damaged window or painting the exterior of the house. Last July, I would much rather have spent $3,200 on interior decorating than on a new roof. But by the following soggy March I was thrilled I had opted for maintaining the roof. Like it or not, I learned home maintenance starts when escrow closes.

Just as being prepared is part and parcel of responsible home ownership, maintaining our inner house is critical to spiritual living, especially during anxious times. Taking care of our spiritual home includes maintaining God's perspective so that we can love God and one another. To put it simply, people going through anxious times need to get—and keep—the big picture. Simple living includes looking to the end, to Jesus' return, so we can get perspective on the present. Living simply is maintaining God's perspective.

Earlier we saw how anxiety turns us into vigilantes, always on the lookout for something terrible to happen to ourselves or someone we love. Jesus would have us be vigilant as well—with a difference. Each of us is like the home owner always on the look out for a thief, but the thief is Jesus. We are to expect Christ's unexpected return. A well-maintained spiritual home is one in which the home owner lives in a constant state of readiness for something both surprising and wonderful.

I have two married friends whose spiritual home is very well-maintained. Jeffrey and Carol are simple people—not in the sense that they are daft or somehow inferior, but in the sense that they live always expecting the best, expecting Jesus' unexpected return. I had the great privilege of living in their basement apartment for five years. It was great fun to be around them. Old "doom and gloom" me began to see there was another way to live. Did Jeffrey and Carol live in a constant state of uninterrupted bliss? Absolutely not. Did all their problems go away? Not a chance. Did they ever suffer from anxiety? Oh yes. But unlike me, Jeffrey and Carol try to maintain God's perspective and live each day simply, thankfully, and full of grace.

A Well-Loved Home

After this he [Jesus] went out and saw a tax collector named Levi, sitting at the tax booth; and he said to him, "Follow me." And he got up, left everything, and followed him.   Luke 5:27–28

This passage in Luke never ceases to amaze me. It all happens so fast. Jesus sees Levi, a member of the fraternity of tax collectors, a group generally despised throughout human history. Even worse, Levi is a Jew collecting taxes for the Romans and that makes him a traitor to his own people. But Levi is tough as nails. As a social and religious outcast, he has had to develop a thick skin over the years in order to survive. Yet Jesus takes one look at him, says a couple of words, and Levi simply drops everything to follow him. What happened? Levi fell in love. As Jesus approached the tax booth, his eyes met Levi's. In an instant, Levi saw in Jesus' eyes a love both deep and vast. Simple love made Levi set out on a new, uncertain life to follow Jesus. Levi had traded in his tax booth for a journey home with Jesus.

Late one night I'm reading in the living room. There's a fire in the fireplace. I'm wrapped in a throw rug, snuggled down in my big chair, two cats in my lap. All is quiet and cozy. For a moment, I think I hear a rattle at the long casement window beside the fireplace. Just the wind, I decide. Then suddenly the window bursts open and with a crash Jesus enters the room. What does he find? A simple soul inhabiting a well-built, well-swept, well-maintained house? Maybe. Maybe not. I do my best to live simply and love God and my neighbor. I try to live with Jesus as Lord, expecting his return. But by no means am I entirely successful. Then I remember the Christ who finds me has the last word—and the last word is love, always love, forever love. Whether I'm wild with worry or living in God's presence, Jesus holds out his arms filled with love and grace, forgiveness and quietness.

CHAPTER 2

the Dining Room:
Gratitude

*When the hour came, he took his place at the table,
and the apostles with him. He said to them, "I have
eagerly desired to eat this Passover with you before I suffer; for I tell you, I will not eat it until it is fulfilled in
the kingdom of God." Then he took a cup, and after
giving thanks he said, "Take this and divide it among
yourselves; for I tell you that from now on I will not
drink of the fruit of the vine until the kingdom of God
comes." Then he took a loaf of bread, and when he had
given thanks, he broke it and gave it to them, saying,
"This is my body, which is given for you. Do this in re-
membrance of me."*   Luke 22:14–19

I enter my dining room through an archway from the living
room. Like the living room it is painted a pale yellow with a
white ceiling. A faux 1920s chandelier hangs over the trestle-
style oak dining table; a matching sideboard stands against
the wall. On the wall opposite, spring sunlight streams

through two large, double-hung windows. On that same wall hangs my colorful collection of decorative plates, depicting scenes of European peasant villages, farms, and vineyards.

I may live alone, but I don't dine alone. When I sit down to supper, I sit down with Jesus. The presence of food, one of the most basic requirements for life, symbolizes the presence of our life-giving God. I breathe a simple prayer of thanks for God's providence. "Give us this day our daily bread," prays the Lord. And God does. To me, the provision of food is an everyday miracle. And I am grateful.

Now I'm no Rebecca of Sunnybrook Farm—just ask any of my friends! If there's a dark side to a person or situation, I'll find it. Of course, like any self-respecting pessimist, I see myself as a hardheaded realist. That's why I so love this Scripture passage from Luke. It is a hardheaded realist's approach to a life of gratitude—in the midst of death and darkness there is reason to return thanks. On the evening before his suffering and death (an anxious time if ever there was one), Jesus is *grateful*. The scene is a dining room. It is Passover, a time to remember slavery's sufferings and a time to celebrate God's liberation. Jesus returns thanks for the bread and the wine, portents of his suffering and liberation to come. The bread is Jesus' broken body, the wine is hope in the kingdom of God.

Being grateful is no Pollyanna-like response to anxious times. For most of us, the daily practice of gratitude begins at mealtimes. For many households, it is not necessarily the calmest, most serene time of day. Frazzled from working all day, Mom has to come up with a healthy, nutritious meal in less than thirty minutes. Dad isn't in such great shape himself; after the stress of the office, he tries to maintain order among fussy, hungry kids. When everyone finally sits down to supper, Sis is sulky, the baby's bawling, and her brother is trying to tell everybody about his day at school, two decibels above his baby sister. "Let us now be thankful. . . ." Right.

But that's where real gratitude begins. Not when life is peaceful and serene, but when everything's falling apart and the resulting anxiety is enough to drive you right through your eyeballs. For anxious people, being grateful to God is a miracle. Simple gratitude helps us experience God at work in every moment of every day. Being grateful doesn't necessarily rescue us from whatever is making us anxious. Instead, gratitude immerses us in the details of everyday life, where God is waiting to meet us.

The old saying is true, God *is* in the details. Oddly, it is in the details of everyday life that we find the big picture, God's perspective. And, as we've already seen, perspective is what we need to acquire during anxious times. It is because Jesus is Lord of the vast, incomprehensible universe that he is also here in the small, seemingly insignificant events and people who make up our lives.

Remember, I'm not preaching a behind-every-cloud-is-a-silver-lining gospel. Living a grateful life is being thankful to God even when everything is falling apart.

I changed careers three times during the past four years. Each career change was preceded by periods of unemployment lasting between five and nine months. As a single person, I didn't have access to another income while I was unemployed. I lived by my wits, doing some freelance work to supplement my unemployment benefits and help make ends meet while I looked for another job. It was at my dining room table, its surface covered in bills, that I learned the power of gratitude. There I would sit, my skinny little checkbook in hand, bills spread all around, and decide which Peter needed to be robbed to pay which Paul. Each time I signed a check and sealed it in an envelope, I prayed a heartfelt prayer of thanks to God for his providence. Gratitude ushered me into the presence of God. Those long, dark, anxiety-filled months of unemployment were lightened by gratitude to God for keeping my head above water. Ever since then, paying my bills has become a time to be grateful instead of a time to complain.

One Out of Ten Lepers

On the way to Jerusalem Jesus was going through the region between Samaria and Galilee. As he entered a village, ten lepers approached him. Keeping their distance, they called out, saying, "Jesus, Master, have mercy on us!" When he saw them, he said to them, "Go and show yourselves to the priests." And as they went, they were made clean. Then one of them, when he saw that he was healed, turned back, praising God with a loud voice. He prostrated himself at Jesus' feet and thanked him. And he was a Samaritan. Then Jesus asked, "Were not ten made clean? But the other nine, where are they? Was none of them found to return and give praise to God except this foreigner?" Then he said to him, "Get up and go on your way; your faith has made you well." Luke 17:11–19

We usually use the word "infidel" to describe someone who is foreign to the faith or a nonbeliever. But in Islam, an infidel is first and foremost anyone who is ungrateful. In Islam it is impossible to believe in Allah and remain ungrateful. It is because an infidel is ungrateful that he is not a true believer and, therefore, a foreigner or outsider.

Jesus was on his way to Jerusalem, the place where he himself would be charged as an infidel condemned to die outside the city. Jesus was traveling between Galilee and Samaria. A sleepy backwater in the Roman Empire, Galilee was home mostly to poor folk and occasional rabble-rousers. Samaria, on the other hand, was inhabited by infidels—non-Jews, foreigners to the faith.

Ten lepers met Jesus on the way. These outsiders were keeping their distance, begging to be healed. Instead of healing them immediately, Jesus sent them to the priests. As the lepers went on their way, they found they had been made clean. But only one out of the ten returned to give Jesus thanks. "And he was a Samaritan." An infidel. An unbeliever. An outsider. And his faith made him well. The foreigner, the infidel, had come home.

It is ambiguous from Luke's account just exactly how the lepers were healed. Jesus didn't touch them or tell them they were healed. He did what any good Jewish teacher would do—he sent them to the professionals, the priests. The lepers were healed somewhere between seeing Jesus and the priests. Are we supposed to think, at first anyway, that the priests had something to do with the healing? But the Samaritan leper was the only one who discerned that God was the source of his healing, not the priests, so he returned to give thanks. In questioning the other lepers' whereabouts, Jesus questions their fidelity, their faithfulness. The implication is clear. The real infidels are the ungrateful, unfaithful lepers still on the road, traveling away from the source of their healing, away from Christ. A miracle made all the lepers clean, but only faith made the grateful Samaritan *well*, an infidel no more.

Fidelity and gratitude are inseparable. Gratitude flows from our deep abiding faith in the mercy of God in Jesus Christ. However, as the story of the lepers demonstrates, gratitude isn't necessarily a natural response to God's mercy and grace. Nine of the lepers never thought to return thanks for their healing. What about us anxious types? Caught up in worry and vain imaginings, I don't always see the mercy of God at work in my life. It sounds corny, but during anxious times we need to "count our blessings, one by one." Simply returning thanks for even one blessing restores us to God's perspective.

A Doorway to Heaven

Jesus went through one town and village after another, teaching as he made his way to Jerusalem. Someone asked him, "Lord, will only a few be saved?" He said to them, "Strive to enter through the narrow door; for many, I tell you, will try to enter and will not be able. When once the owner of the house has got up and shut the door, and you begin to stand outside and to knock at the door, saying, 'Lord, open to us,' then in reply he will say to you, 'I do not know where you come from.' Then you will begin to say, 'We ate and drank with you, and you taught in our streets.' But he will say, 'I do not know where you come from; go away from me, all you evildoers!' There will be weeping and gnashing of teeth when you see Abraham and Isaac and Jacob and all the prophets in the kingdom of God and you yourselves thrown out. Then people will come from east and west, from north and south, and will eat in the

> *kingdom of God. Indeed, some are last who will be first,*
> *and some are first who will be last."*
>
> Luke 13:22–30

This passage follows closely two other passages about the kingdom of God. Jesus compares God's kingdom to a mustard seed that grows into a large tree. He then further compares the kingdom of God to yeast that a woman uses to make bread rise. We find God's kingdom in the smallest places.

Jesus now tells how hard it is to enter the narrow door in answer to the question, "Lord, will only a few be saved?" The questioners are probably already believers who think they're in like Flynn. Surprise. God, the Homeowner, doesn't recognize any of the people claiming a prior acquaintance. There's a dinner party to end all dinner parties going on in God's kingdom, and some don't make the A list—or the B list. "Indeed, some are last who will be first, and some are first who will be last." Like the encounter with the lepers, those who are out are in, and those who are in are out.

Jesus is still on his way to Jerusalem, the place he will suffer and die. Of course, part of entering the narrow door to God's kingdom involves suffering for the sake of the gospel. But there's much more on the other side of the door. There's mercy, grace, resurrection. The door may be small, but inside there's a big party going on for those with the eyes to see, the ears to hear.

There's so much more to salvation than just being saved. Jesus saves once and for all. Yet we enjoy our salvation now. I think that's another part of what Jesus tells us throughout the gospels: the kingdom of God is both now and in the time to come. Don't worry about kingdom come. But don't miss the kingdom of God here, in your midst, because there's a feast going on. Just look for the small, narrow door and knock.

Gratitude is the knock on the door. Giving thanks summons the Homeowner. Living a grateful life is the art of paying attention to the details, of taking nothing for granted, and returning thanks for the smallest, the most hidden of God's blessings. We anxious types need all the blessings we can get. But first we need to find them. The blessings are there. Our blessings may be small or entirely hidden from view, but in them we find the door to God's kingdom.

I don't believe all dreams come with a message from God. Some do. But then, I'm no Joseph and, in my experience, such dreams are rare. In fact, I've really only experienced one dream that, upon waking, I felt in my heart was God speaking to me. At the time I was unemployed. God's message for my next career was hidden in the dream, and I would end up following a career path I never dreamed of following. The path would be a way filled with God's hidden blessings.

Eventually I found a job in marketing for a large bank. Banking was the last career I would have imagined for myself. My image of a bank had always been that of stuffy, humorless men in identical suits working in vast, windowless rooms, and everyone speaking in hushed tones. How boring. Even worse, the business of banking is money—dreaded "mammon." Checking accounts. Savings accounts. CDs. Home loans. Credit—"usury." In short, I couldn't think of a duller, less spiritual pursuit than banking.

But after six months on the job, I found myself wishing I'd discovered banking twenty years earlier. Not only did I meet incredibly interesting and bright people at the bank, but I became intrigued by how banks move money throughout the world. My job involved marketing financial services to corporations around the world. It had nothing to do with boring old checking and savings accounts and everything to do with the fascinating world of multinational banking: investment banking, international trade, project finance, cash management, private banking, and other global banking services I never dreamed existed. Oh, to be an investment banker—how interesting, how challenging, how lucrative!

With the unexpected pleasure of delighting in my new banking career, I thought my dream had come true. And my new career in banking enabled me to buy my first home—yet another hidden blessing revealed. Surely that was what God was showing me in the dream. But there was more.

My parents and I had never been particularly close.

Because I had not married, had children, or settled down in a particular career, I don't think they ever saw me as a grown-up. For the most part, I didn't include them in any major decisions I made; I just announced to them what I was going to do next.

Then I bought a house. I had finally taken on a major adult responsibility—a mortgage. Buying the house committed me to working at the bank for the foreseeable future. Months later, my mother told me how proud my dad was of me for taking on the responsibilities of owning my own home.

My parents were very supportive during that anxious time of buyer's remorse. They came to my house every weekend to help. Dad installed new doors, a new bathroom sink, window treatments, and a garbage disposal. He put a new roof on the garden porch and built an armoire from a kit. He drilled countless holes, painted, sanded, nailed, and caulked. Mom brought food—lots of it. Both told me not to worry—the house was adorable, it had resale potential. They told me I didn't have to do everything at once (even though I did anyway). That first year of home ownership brought me closer to my parents than ever before, and I am grateful for such a surprising blessing.

In the last chapter we looked at how anxiety turns us into vigilantes, always expecting the worst. Looking for blessings is being vigilant in a different way; instead of expecting the worst, we expect to find God's blessings everyday. Searching daily for our blessings gets us off the treadmill of worry and liberates us to thank and praise God.

Anxious people can't afford to look a gift horse in the mouth. To put it more spiritually, there is no such thing as a small blessing. It's the small, hidden blessings that will see us anxious types through the day.

I have a friend at work whose anxiety level is off the charts. She makes *me* seem relaxed. She expresses her quest for small blessings this way: "I hope something nice happens today." My friend says that everyday. It is a kind of prayer. And very often something nice does happen. We have fun working on a project together; we walk outside to a beautiful California-perfect day; a long, afternoon meeting is canceled; the boss says, "Good work!" Small, nice things are blessings. My friend is grateful to God for each one. And upon finding another of God's blessings, she is a little less anxious than before.

Anxiety's darkness cannot overpower the small, hidden blessings of God. They are the doorway to his kingdom. So pay attention to the details, look for God there, and when you find him, be thankful.

Living gratefully can help eliminate several underlying causes of anxiety. I've often found the source of my anxiety lies in one of the seven deadly sins: envy, greed, lust, gluttony, anger, pride, and sloth. Out of these seven, envy is most frequently the cause of great anxiety. And out of the sin of envy comes greed, lust, gluttony, anger, and pride. Sloth has its own peculiar way of producing anxiety.

The Uninvited House Guests: Envy and Anger

Envy has got to be the most deadly sin. Comparisons are indeed odious. When we compare ourselves with others, envy gets a toehold in our spiritual houses. Envy gets a full foot in the door when our comparisons show that we somehow lack something or someone in our lives. Envy quietly slips through the door when we begin to want what others have. And we begin to worry and fret over what's missing in our lives or, worse, plot how to get what others have. Envy makes its way to the dining room to serve up generous helpings of greed, lust, gluttony, anger, or pride.

My first year of home ownership was dominated by my fear and anxiety over crime in the neighborhood. Just four months after I moved in, my next-door neighbors' house was broken into by burglars. My neighbors have an alarm system similar to mine. It is triggered when magnets in the doors and windows are disturbed by someone trying to gain entry. The burglars circumvented this problem by merely kicking in a thin, wooden panel in the back door—the door itself was never opened, so the alarm didn't sound. They then carried their loot through the hole in the door to a waiting Mercedes Benz parked in the driveway.

And something worse was about to happen. Two months after the burglary, a serial rapist struck my neighborhood and the more upscale neighborhood adjacent to mine. Five single women living alone were each sexually assaulted by a man who kicked in the doors of their homes. One woman lived on the next block behind my house. I felt like a sitting duck. (Now you know why I installed security doors!) It was three months before the rapist was finally caught. I don't believe I've ever known such fear before. I was out of my mind with constant, uninterrupted anxiety.

With burglary and rape, could murder be far behind? As I worried and fretted over what sort of crime spree would hit my neighborhood next, I kept telling myself that these things happen in the best of neighborhoods. Prior to buying my house, I lived in a small, elegant cottage in a swank, expensive neighborhood in the Oakland hills. I rarely worried about crime during the five years I lived there.

During my first year of home ownership I missed that cottage—a lot. Two weeks after I moved into my new house, my old landlord phoned to tell me what happened in my former backyard. He came home to find police helicopters flying low over his house and my old cottage. As he got closer, he saw police cars had surrounded his property. Getting out of his car, he was informed by the police that an armed and dangerous man was hiding somewhere on the property. Several hours later the police caught the criminal, who was high on heroin and carrying an assault rifle. Mind you, all of this took place in one of the best neighborhoods in the Bay Area. Still, it was mighty cold comfort to know that crime can strike anywhere.

But it was during the four months the burglary and rapes took place that envy quietly moved in to make me even more anxious. I began to believe that married people with homes in better neighborhoods were safer and happier than I. Riding home on the bus from my job in San Francisco, I would stare at the affluent commuters around me. They were all headed for their beautiful, expensive homes in the relative safety of the Oakland hills. They didn't have to go home to an empty, dark house in a dicey neighborhood such as mine. Oh no. They all had loving spouses to welcome them to their bright and cheerful homes. I was green with envy because they had what I didn't have—a gorgeous home filled with a loving family in a safe neighborhood.

Not much later, envy began to serve me large helpings of anger and greed. I became resentful. After all, why should I have to suffer just because I couldn't afford to buy in the hills? Not only was I envious, but I grew increasingly angry about my tragic lot in life. Then came greed. I began to plot how I would sell my house the following spring. I worked out how much the sales price would be and marked it up another ten percent. I deserved a much better house in a neighborhood free of crime. I began clipping newspaper ads selling luxury townhomes. I went on a huge home improvement binge—not because it pleased me, but because home improvements would bring me a bigger return when I put the house on the market.

Did any of this plotting and home improvement lessen

my anxiety about crime in my neighborhood? No. Instead, envy and its companion, anger, only fueled my anxious feelings, which soared to new, astronomical levels. Envy and anger only made me feel worse, and the resulting anxiety didn't solve a thing.

Greed, Lust, Gluttony, and Pride

Though envy and anger were my favorite sins during that awful time, greed, lust, gluttony, and pride are also spawned from envy. They can take up residence just as easily when we begin to feel our lives are somehow less than full or that we're missing something.

Lust, greed, and gluttony are like triplets. Lust is greedy for people; greed is a glutton for money and things; gluttony lusts after food and drink. And these sins are never satisfied. The emptiness is never filled. Lust, greed, and gluttony always demand more. And that's when anxiety really takes off. Anxiety rockets when we get what or who we want—and its *still not enough*. We become increasingly anxious over how to get more money, sex, possessions, love, food, time, recognition, happiness, security, freedom, beauty, power (control), or whatever it takes to fill the void.

And then there's pride. In a way, pride is the flip side of envy. Just as envy begins with odious comparisons, so does pride. Pride often exists at the expense of someone else. It looks at others and finds what's missing or inferior about them to make us feel superior in some way. American literature is filled with stories about proud men "who don't take nothin' from nobody." Though the stories may cast such heroes in the lowliest of circumstances, their pride is often rooted in a sense of moral superiority. As admirable a trait as independence is, when it is sustained by pride, it exists because other people are diminished or lessened in some way.

Then there are the "house proud." Keeping a well-maintained home is the foundation of responsible home ownership. In a positive way, keeping a house maintained and clean is a healthy source of pride. But pride can become diseased. One day the proud homeowner looks up and down the street and compares his house with other houses on the block. Compared to his, some of the homes aren't nearly as well kept, and a few are even in deplorable condition. The homeowner's heart swells with pride.

Of course, that homeowner is me. It wasn't enough for me to maintain my home as best I could and make it an attractive, comfortable place in which to live. Oh no. In order to ease my anxiety about whether I got a good deal on the house and whether I'd be able to sell it when the time came, I looked next door for comparison and found it deeply wanting. My neighbors' house was on the market the same time my house was for sale. So I toured the house next door by way of comparison. Just like my house, it is a California bungalow with the same floor plan but different architectural details. What a dump. The owners had moved in ten years before and simply pitched camp. Except for new external (and unattractive) paint, nothing had been improved on the house for at least a decade. The thousand-square-foot house was crammed with ten years of stuff for three people. The small backyard was full of dead grass, as was the front yard. Forget landscaping. A dog much too large for the house and yard lay sleeping, surrounded by junk, on a cleared patch of floor in the living room. Dirty dishes were everywhere. Piles of dirty laundry were scattered around the basement, where the washer and dryer were kept. The only thing missing was a rusted-out car parked out front. My neighbors' house never did sell.

After touring their house I nicknamed my soon-to-be neighbors "Ma and Pa Kettle." The name stuck as I worried through my first year of home ownership. My favorite Ma and Pa Kettle story was the husband's brief attempt to garden. Pa Kettle finally stopped watching television to venture outdoors one day. He walked to the garage and pulled out his lawn mower. Pa turned the mower on and revved it up with much noise and fanfare. With a little swagger in his step, the master of the house then proceeded to mow a little dead grass and a lot of bone-dry dust and dirt in the front and back yards. The whole exercise took less than ten minutes. For the life of me, I couldn't see how the lawns were improved under the mower. To this day, I've never seen Pa mow the lawns again.

I used my neighbors as a landmark for comparison during my death drive to improve my own home that first year. I couldn't make improvements fast enough—new paint, new drapes, new area carpets, new furniture, new doors, new tile in the kitchen and bathroom, new gardens in front and back. I made Martha Stewart look like a piker. No matter what I did to my house, I'd tell myself, anything will improve its value over Ma and Pa Kettle's.

I was sick with pride. I had diminished my neighbors (and de-humanized them with a nasty name) to make me feel less anxious about spending so much money so fast on home improvements. Did priding myself over my neighbors relieve my anxiety and gnawing buyer's remorse? No, it certainly did not. Did it make me a fool every time I called them Ma and Pa Kettle? Indeed it did.

Envy begins with odious comparisons and shows us that, compared to others, we don't have enough and resent what others have. What begins as envy results in anger, lust, greed, gluttony, and pride. These sins whisper promises to fill the emptiness envy creates. But such promises are empty because there is never enough of anything or anyone to fill the void.

So there I was, terrified that everybody had a nicer house than mine and spending money like a drunken sailor on home improvements. I worked furiously on my house, convinced that if I could make the house better it might be good enough—someday. By that time, I was up to my neck in at least five of the seven deadly sins—all urging me to want what others have and resent them for it, work harder, get more money, spend more money, and look down upon neighbors less industrious than myself. Exhausted after a day full of hard work, I sat down to supper one night and just stared at my plate. I was gripped by a paralyzing anxiety. All I could do was say, "Oh my God, what have I done?" (This referred not to the many sins I committed during the day, but to deep remorse at having bought the house in the first place.)

Surprisingly, God answered me. Scales fell from my eyes. For the first time, I really saw the food on my plate. I don't remember now exactly what kind of food it was, only that it was a simple meal I'd thrown together quickly. While I stared at my plate, my mind filled with Jesus' words, "Give us this day our daily bread." And it was enough. What more could I possibly want? Nothing. That evening's supper was all I had any right to ask of God. Anxiety melted before the warmth of God's providence. And I was grateful, deeply grateful. The resulting prayer was as simple as the meal—"Thank you, God. Thank you."

Sloth

There is one more deadly sin to consider briefly. Though sloth is not directly related to its six sister sins, it is still counted among them—like the evil stepsister in a fairy tale.

"Sloth" is such an old-fashioned word. It's easy to see

why sloth may have been a problem for past generations when life was simpler and slower. Surely nobody in today's world has time for sloth. But in the twentieth century, sloth most commonly disguises itself in contemporary dress—procrastination. Procrastination's maxim is "always put off today what you can do tomorrow."

It has taken me four days to write the last two paragraphs. I had plenty of time to write with nothing better to do; but somehow I just never got around to writing. Instead, I filled in some holes in the wall for a painting project that wouldn't begin for four weeks. I took a nap. I wandered around and tidied up my already-neat-as-a-pin house. I adjusted the motion detector on the floodlights over the garage. In desperation, I played with the cats. I had to actually work at finding dull things to do so I could continue to avoid writing.

The week before, I placed some significant modifications to this book on a computer disk, which mysteriously disappeared. I couldn't go on writing the book without the disk. I spent an hour searching the house for it. I was angry with myself for misplacing it, saying to myself, "I was *really* ready to write this time. Why, I could've written a whole chapter this very evening, if only I hadn't lost that disk!" I was about to give up when a small voice inside my head said, "Look in the garbage can." I went through the garbage, piece by piece. And there it was on the very bottom. I must have scooped it up while I tidied the study and thrown the disk away with some junk mail. The disk was a little smelly but otherwise in perfect condition. I could procrastinate no longer.

While I was busy doing mind-numbing things around the house, my anxiety escalated over whether I'd be able to finish the book in time. The more I put it off, the harder it was to sit down and work. I kept making promises to myself that I would write—later. The longer I procrastinated, the more anxious I became. The more anxious I became, the more paralyzed I got about getting started. The more paralyzed I became about getting started, the longer I procrastinated. Does any of this have a familiar ring?

That's what makes sloth such a deadly sin. Masquerading as procrastination, it can generate a kind of paralyzing anxiety that ultimately prevents us from doing what God is calling us to do. And the inactivity that results can eventually hurt not only ourselves but those who depend on us. For example, as important to me as it was to finish the book on time, it was even more important to my publisher—who already allocated financial and human resources to publish the book by a predetermined date. My publisher depended on me to finish the book by its deadline. Other jobs than mine were involved; indulging in slothful procrastination would only eventually hurt sales, revenues, and the ability of other people to do their jobs effectively. Sloth hurts. It distracts us from doing whatever God is calling us to do.

All life is a gift from God. The seven deadly sins deceive us into believing that God's gifts are really objects we can control to suit our own purposes. They deceive us into believing that if we can be like the Jones's, get more money or love, delay doing what needs to be done, etc., etc., we can relax. Instead, the more we indulge in the seven deadly sins, the more anxiety escalates to new levels. But if we can view all of life as a gift from God, rest in God's mercy and providence alone, and be grateful for enough and more than enough, the seven deadly sins lose their power over us and anxiety melts under the grace and love of God.

It's easy to see how gratitude to God helps us cope during anxious times. But that is only part of living a grateful life. Out of gratitude to God flows gratitude to others. During times of severe stress and high anxiety, expressing our thanks to people who love and support us can help break up the loneliness anxiety creates. Anxiety shuts us off from others. We become so concerned with our worries it's tempting to believe "nobody knows the trouble I've seen." Expressing gratitude to family and friends who are helpful and supportive reconnects us to the real world and relieves our anxious minds of the misbelief that we are all alone.

On October 17, 1989, at 5:04 P.M., an earthquake registering 7.1 on the Richter scale struck the greater San Francisco Bay Area. Thousands lost their homes, and more than sixty people lost their lives. The Oakland Bay Bridge was severely damaged, stranding hundreds of commuters in San Francisco. My Oakland neighborhood escaped serious damage to homes, but one neighbor was injured badly when the freeway collapsed underneath his car. For most of us, the earthquake immediately separated us from friends and family at the office or commuting on the way home. With no telephone service, we had no idea where they were, whether they were injured or alive. (When phone service was restored two days later, I learned that my coworkers believed I had died underneath an Oakland freeway on my way home.) As tremors continued to jolt the Bay Area, I'm convinced that every single resident was out of his mind with anxiety. And yet it was in the middle of this catastrophe that incredibly anxious people were grateful to equally anxious strangers who helped in so many ways: putting out the fires in the Marina; helping rescue the injured from the Oakland freeway collapse; giving people shelter when their damaged homes were condemned; helping each other find alternative routes home; and huddling together and telling each other it was going to be okay. We were all in this together and we helped and supported each other the best we could. Every act to help a neighbor or stranger was an act of heroism. What I remember especially was how often people expressed their thanks to one another. That expression of gratitude helped with the terrible anxiety we all felt.

When we think we can't stand any more trouble, anxiety, or worry, we need to remember to thank the heroes who help, support, and love us. And thank God for them.

On the eve of his death, Jesus returned thanks in an upstairs dining room. We follow Jesus. Faced with seemingly overwhelming anxiety, we, too, can thank God for his providence and blessings in our lives this anxious day and for his hope in the life to come.

Chicken. Broccoli. Rice. I place another uninspired supper on the dining room table. The house is very quiet. Staring at my plate, I begin to feel just a bit sorry for myself—another meal to eat alone. With a little sigh, I bow my head to say grace. "Lord, for the gift of this food make me truly thankful. Amen." A warm evening breeze moves through the open window. Lifting my head and my fork at the same time, I see Jesus gazing at me with solemn eyes. Before him is a simple earthen platter upon which rests unleavened bread. A small shallow bowl holds a dark-red wine. Jesus raises his as yet unwounded hands in blessing. I understand. The journey is far from over. There is much more to come. More anxious times. More rich blessings. But now, tonight, this supper is ours. And we pray, "Give us this day our daily bread." Amen and amen.

CHAPTER 3

the Kitchen: Hospitality

One of the Pharisees asked Jesus to eat with him, and he went into the Pharisee's house and took his place at the table. And a woman in the city, who was a sinner, having learned that he was eating in the Pharisee's house, brought an alabaster jar of ointment. She stood behind him at his feet, weeping, and began to bathe his feet with her tears and to dry them with her hair. Then she continued kissing his feet and anointing them with the ointment. Now when the Pharisee who had invited him saw it, he said to himself, "If this man were a prophet, he would have known who and what kind of woman this is who is touching him—that she is a sinner." . . . Then turning toward the woman, [Jesus] said to Simon, "Do you see this woman? I entered your house; you gave me no water for my feet, but she has bathed my feet with her tears and dried them with her hair. You gave me no kiss, but from the time I came in she has not stopped kissing my feet. You did not anoint my head with oil, but she has anointed my feet

> *with ointment. Therefore, I tell you, her sins, which*
> *were many, have been forgiven; hence she has shown*
> *great love. But the one to whom little is forgiven, loves*
> *little." Then he said to her, "Your sins are forgiven."*
>   Luke 7:36–39; 44–48

*A*bout three days after I moved into my new house, I was standing on the porch outside my kitchen door, surveying my new, but sadly neglected, garden. As I tried to figure out how to make the garden bloom again, I happened to look up over the back fence and see an abandoned, boarded-up house looming above my garden. On first seeing it, my heart sank to my toes. I don't know how I could possibly have missed seeing such a large, ugly structure in the neighborhood. *That's it,* I thought to myself. *I'll never be able to resell my house now.*

A few days later, I mentioned the abandoned house to my next-door neighbors. They informed me that since the house had been abandoned, it had become a "crack house." It had been there ever since they moved in six years ago. The neighborhood had for years tried to get the city to tear the house down, to no avail. As I listened, a fresh, piercing wave of anxiety washed over me. It was bad enough to have an eyesore detracting from the value of my home, but the reality that I actually lived so close to the neighborhood's local crime magnet made me reel. Of course, I was sick with worry even though there was nothing I could do. Eventually I decided the only way I could regain my sanity was to ignore the crack house completely. I simply pretended it wasn't there.

Four months later, I was awakened at two in the morning by the sound of chain saws and trucks driving up and down my street. I got up to look out my front window to see what was going on, but I saw nothing. Still sleepy, I went back to bed assuming the phone company was doing some repair work in the neighborhood. In my semiconscious state I never thought to wonder how the phone company might be fixing the lines with chain saws.

As I went to work the next morning, one of my next-door neighbors leaned out of his kitchen window and asked if I'd heard all the excitement. I had a dim memory of chain saws. He yelled, "There was a big fire in the crack house last night." I looked up to see a few remaining charred trees (that explained the chain saws) and the half-burned upper story of the crack house. A two-alarm fire had raged close to my house and I had been oblivious to the danger. As close as the fire was, my home and my neighbors' homes had escaped damage. As I got into my car to head for the train, I kept praying, "Thank you, God. Thank you."

Six months later the city finally tore down the half-burned crack house. A happy ending to yet another hair-raising experience as a new home owner. Long after the crack house's demise, I still think about the incident and I am reminded that not every house is a home. Too many people grow up in houses where there is substance abuse or physical abuse. Instead of containing love and warmth, such houses are filled with anxiety, fear, and violence. They are frighteningly inhospitable, to say the least.

Jesus once found himself in an inhospitable house. But there is a delightful irony to Jesus' experience. He went to dinner at the house of a Pharisee, a Jew dedicated to pursuing holiness and religious purity. We might call the Pharisee a saint.

The Pharisee's house should have been a home. Instead, his house was in a state of spiritual abandonment and decay. When Jesus arrived, no hospitality was extended to him—until a sinner showed up unannounced. With wild abandon, the woman put soothing ointment on Jesus. She bathed and repeatedly kissed his feet. Common hospitality, which should have been offered by the Pharisee, was made extravagant by the woman's unspoken love for Jesus. It was a sinner who made the Pharisee's house a home, a place inhabited by the forgiveness of God.

It's not immediately clear who's being hospitable to whom. Urged by great love, the woman certainly lavishes hospitality on Jesus. But there's more to the incident than first meets the eye. Jesus' words are for the Pharisee only: "Therefore, I tell you, her sins, which were many, have been forgiven; hence she has shown great love. But the one to whom little is forgiven, loves little." He doesn't withhold forgiveness from the Pharisee; instead Jesus simply points out the spiritual poverty of the Pharisee's house.

Where there is little to forgive, there is little love. Jesus and the sinner have made the Pharisee's house a hospitable home by filling it with the loving presence of extravagant grace. It seems to me that the Pharisee is as much a beneficiary of hospitality as Jesus. Neither the Pharisee nor the woman (sinner) are named. As readers, we are left with the feeling that we, too, are both the sinner and saint, equally unworthy recipients of Jesus' graceful hospitality.

Hospitality is a grand gesture of acceptance. Christ's hospitality is forgiveness and acceptance. It welcomes friends and family, strangers and sinners. Because we live in Christ, the hospitality with which we welcome others is generated by a deep, passionate, single-minded love of Jesus extended to all comers. Hospitality comes from the heart, Christ's true home.

Living a hospitable life is a perpetual celebration of Advent. We are always expecting to see Jesus. I like the ancient monastic practice of welcoming each guest as Christ. Monastic hospitality celebrates guests as though they were Christ come again. Now that's hospitality!

It's a Good Thing

When we extend hospitality, we give the gift of ourselves in anticipation of our guests. When she saw Jesus, the woman gave of herself, bathing Jesus' feet with her tears and hair.

When we receive guests, such a welcome may be just a little excessive. But the gift of ourselves is a good thing expressed in the hospitality we extend. I think that is the secret of Martha Stewart's success. She doesn't just teach us how to entertain, but she shows us how to give a little extra bit of ourselves in everything we do, which is at the heart of genuine hospitality.

Mind you, as much as I enjoy Martha Stewart's magazine, books, and TV shows, the woman exhausts me. I'd have to quit my job to do everything Martha advises. But living a hospitable life is not about getting exhausted and stressed out over making special preparations for guests. When anxious people like me offer hospitality, the gifts we give of ourselves should be simple. Remember, keeping it simple is key.

The best Christmas Eve I ever had was very simple. Another single friend of mine and I did not have family obligations, so we decided to spend Christmas Eve together at my house. I wanted the evening to be special, but I wanted to enjoy it, too, instead of working myself to death over an elaborate menu and preparations. I decided to keep it simple but elegant. When my friend Jamie arrived, the house was candlelit, a fire glowed in the fireplace, and the small Christmas tree shone brightly. The dining table was set with my everyday green dinnerware made elegant with white linen napkins and crystal stemware. Red carnations with sprigs of green leaves in a cut-crystal vase made the centerpiece. Next to the table sat a huge glass flower vase filled with ice and a bottle of sparkling cider. On the menu were barbecued steaks, baked potatoes, salad, and a simple dessert. I poured Jamie a glass of cider and made her comfortable in the kitchen while I made the few preparations necessary for dinner. The evening was a wonderful success. I actually relaxed! We talked and talked about everything, enjoyed a marvelous dinner, exchanged gifts, and listened to Christmas music on the stereo. Jamie later told me that she went home feeling as celebrated as the season itself.

My Home's True Heart

My kitchen is the heart of my home, architecturally and emotionally. The kitchen is the connecting room between the public areas of the living and dining rooms and the more private areas, the bedrooms and bathroom. The kitchen is larger than most 1920s California bungalows. It is painted white; the molding around the window above the sink and doors are painted the same pale yellow as the walls in the living and dining rooms. The cabinets are constructed of a medium-dark wood. When I moved in, I replaced the gold-flecked Milar countertops and backsplash with white tile; the backsplash shows an occasional tile featuring a small wild-flower. From the ceiling hangs a pot rack with dark green enameled pots hanging from its hooks (my kitchen accessories and small appliances are also dark green, my favorite color). Next to the exit door to the hallway is a hideaway ironing board cupboard that a former owner transformed into a spice cabinet. I removed the door and transformed the old spice cabinet into a display case for decorative plates and tiles. Next to the display case is the door to the half-basement. Then comes the refrigerator (opposite the stove and prep counter on the other wall) and an archway to the breakfast room, an extension of the kitchen.

The breakfast room is painted in the same manner as the kitchen proper. However, it was there I made my first decorating error. I painted the old, built-in hutch green—a dark green that makes the hutch look like a large, dark blob on one wall of the breakfast room. I tried to brighten it up a bit by installing big brass knobs in the shape of teacups, teapots, sugar bowls, and creamers. I also added area rugs and a Parisian table with two chairs, also in dark green. It's *really* green in there! Luckily, next to the hutch is the door with a window to the back garden, and on the wall opposite the hutch is another window. Sunlight, more than anything else, softens the dark colors.

I take pains to describe my kitchen because it is such an important room to me. As I mentioned before, anxiety can be a very lonely experience for me. Intense, chronic worry over someone or something tends to blot out the rest of the world. Friends and family can't really help, often because they can't change whatever it is that's driving me to distraction. Even God seems far away, and I feel all alone awash in anxiety, lost in my secret world of plots, scenarios, and other vain imaginings, cut off from those who love me. However, when I step into my kitchen, worries fade.

Though I live alone, the kitchen keeps me busy. Doing something constructive definitely helps me cope with anxiety. The kitchen always seems to need cleaning. Fortunately, I love to clean. Nothing cheers me up like the smell of Pine-Sol, Clorox, Murphy's Oil Soap, or Dawn (Green Mountain Spring). Cleaning takes me out of myself; I can get so involved with cleaning the kitchen that I forget my worries for a while. However, much as I love to clean, it doesn't help much with the loneliness anxiety can bring. I enjoy my kitchen the most, therefore, when I'm preparing dinner there for guests.

Hospitality begins in my kitchen, and not only when I'm preparing a meal. When I invite guests into the kitchen, I accept them as special friends (I put "company" on the couch out in the living room). Hospitality begins when I make guests comfortable in the kitchen. I invite guests to sit in chairs brought in from the breakfast room, then give them something to drink and appetizers to nibble on. As I work to prepare the meal, there is usually much conversation and laughter and everyone pitches in to help. My anxious isolation melts in a kitchen filled with the warmth of good cooking and good friends.

Hospitality is a grand gesture of grace. Living a hospitable life is a way of imitating Christ, the Gracious Host. When we practice hospitality, we practice grace. We accept people for exactly who they are, not for who we would like them to be. Practicing hospitality helps us to let go of that anxious need to control and graciously accept others just as they are.

Random Acts of Kindness

"But love your enemies, do good, and lend, expecting nothing in return. Your reward will be great, and you will be children of the Most High; for he is kind to the ungrateful and the wicked." Luke 6:35–36

There is much more to hospitality than merely entertaining friends for dinner. Entertainment is only a part of what hospitality can offer. The woman who bathed Jesus' feet with ointment and kisses extended hospitality to Jesus that went well beyond entertainment. She was praised for her great love, which caused her to lavish such attention on Jesus. Like the woman at the Pharisee's house, when we practice hospitality we offer the gift of ourselves to friends, family, strangers, and even enemies.

Sometimes I think the closest most of us can ever come to expressing unconditional, *agape* love is through practicing hospitality with simple acts of kindness. In Luke 6:35–36, Jesus shows us how to live hospitably by loving even our enemies with kindness—"do good, and lend, expecting nothing in return." Simple kindness is important to God, who is even "kind to the ungrateful and the wicked." Genuine hospitality is made up of random acts of kindness expressing Christ's grace and acceptance to whomever God puts in our lives.

My boss, Laura, is the most genuinely hospitable person I know. She has managed to incorporate Martha Stewart-like hospitality at work. At Christmas she left a little decorated Christmas tree on each coworker's desk and a cheerful coffee mug filled with homemade cookies, all tied up with bright ribbons. We came to work one Halloween to find treats and special Halloween pencils on our desks. She is always bringing me magazine articles and ideas on decorating the kitchen. I've seen Laura treat everyone with whom she works at the bank with simple kindness. To Laura, nobody is unimportant—from senior executives to mailroom clerks.

But perhaps the kindest thing Laura did was to boost the self-esteem of a colleague. Through political infighting several years ago, one of Laura's colleagues unfairly lost her title of vice president at the bank. Though the lost title entailed no monetary difference to the colleague's present job at the bank, Laura was able to reinstate the woman to the position of vice president. It was an unnecessary, extremely kind and hospitable act.

When we live hospitably and kindly toward whomever God brings into our lives, we give up the compelling need to control people and situations. Practicing random acts of kindness is a way of "keeping our sticky fingers off the controls," says Anne Lamott in *Operating Instructions*.[1] No one can "own" kindness. Like Christ's love, it is given with no strings attached. Even minuscule acts of kindness are released into the hands of our good God, who does what he wills without first checking in with us.

Hospitality is important to God, as we learn in Scripture. In Genesis 18, Abram's hospitality toward God's messengers is recorded carefully with the accounts of the food Sarai prepared and the way in which Abram welcomed the messengers. Abram's hospitality seems to be as important as the message that Sarai will bear a child in old age. In fact, the text shows us that how we welcome God affects how well we hear the message God has for us. Remember the story of Sodom in Genesis 19? That city denied hospitality and decency to strangers, which had a definite impact on the terrifying events that followed.

One of the most touching gestures of hospitality in the Bible is that of a father welcoming home his rebellious son. The older son is practically perfect in every way: he's obedient, never gives his father cause for a sleepless night, and works on the farm like a slave. However, the youngest son is cut from a different cloth. Upon demanding and receiving his portion of the inheritance, the young man immediately sets out to see the world and experience life. Having squandered his inheritance on loose women and fast cars in foreign places, he finds himself homeless and facing starvation. He decides to go home and take what's coming to him. What's coming to him is the surprise of his life.

Just Family

"So he set off and went to his father. But while he was still far off, his father saw him and was filled with compassion; he ran and put his arms around him and kissed him. . . . But the father said to his slaves, 'Quickly, bring out a robe—the best one—and put it on him; put a ring on his finger and sandals on his feet. And get the fatted calf and kill it, and let us eat and celebrate; for this son of mine was dead and is alive again; he was lost and is found!' And they began to celebrate." Luke 15:20; 22–24

I love the New Testament Greek word for "compassion"—*splangnizomai*. The English word is completely inadequate to express the powerful emotion Jesus' parable demands. *Splangnizomai* goes far beyond love; it means to be overwhelmingly moved—literally, to feel your guts turn upside down or to have a gut-wrenching experience. Compassion expressed in prodigal welcome is what the unfaithful son had coming to him. The father's hospitality is all out of proportion to what his young son deserves—at least that's what the more mature, responsible, and not to mention *faithful* son thought. But only a parent can know that volatile mixture of relief, joy (anger), love, and gratitude, which explodes in the heart at the sight of a lost child returned home. So the father expresses the overpowering compassion he feels for his good-for-nothing son by extending him his most heartwarming hospitality.

I find it interesting that Jesus' parable is set in the context of a family. It's almost easy to be hospitable toward friends and guests. But I find offering hospitality to my own family to be a little more difficult. Why? Is it that I take them for granted? Do I share a little too much past history with them, which might include a few unforgiven wrongs, slights, or troubles? Do I think I know them too well, know what they expect, like or dislike? Or perhaps I'm just a little lazy when I welcome them to my home ("Never mind; it's just family.")? If I am at all honest, I must answer "yes" to all the above.

It's easy to take family for granted. After all, they'll always be there, right? Well, maybe. In a day and age when divorce is all too common and grown families are separated by great distances (never mind death and illness), the assumption that family will always be there isn't necessarily a guarantee. I don't mean to make anybody feel guilty. Family may not always be there for us. But while family is still available to us, we mustn't take their presence for granted. Occasionally extending the same kind of hospitality we offer guests helps us to see Christ in the all-too-familiar eyes of family, and we value and treasure them. For anxious people, living hospitably with family is a way of rising above the anxiety for a while to express love and appreciation.

The first holiday season in my new house was memorable. When I was still renting, I never had room to host my entire family for the holidays. For forty years I spent every Christmas holiday at a family member's home. So as soon as I signed the title papers in July, I told the family that year-end holidays would be spent at my house.

I had as much fun getting ready for the holiday (months in advance) as I did when Thanksgiving and Christmas actually arrived. By the time Thanksgiving arrived, the house was scrubbed, polished, and decorated. The winter holidays were filled with good food, laughter, gifts, parents, kids—and the subsequent holiday debris. When it was all over, I felt more relaxed than I had all year. It seemed to me as though the house changed too. As I welcomed my family for the holidays, the house seemed to welcome me as well. Somehow the house seemed more mine, more like I belonged there. The house had become my home.

Oh, sure, you might be saying. It's easy for her to expound on the virtues of living hospitably with family because she lives alone—no husband to leave dirty clothes in a corner of the bedroom; no teenager sulking her way through adolescent angst; no two-year-old demanding constant care; no family crises to come home to. I may not live with my family, but I have been privileged to be the recipient of family-style hospitality and I know how comforting that can be.

Several years ago, while living in southern California, I was going through one of my career changes. Anxiety about my future was unusually high. My friend Alice and her husband, Fred, sort of tacitly "adopted" me. The memories I cherish the most involve the times we just hung out together in their kitchen.

Their kitchen remains the most wonderful room I've ever been in. It was large with lots of plants in the windows. There was always a jumble of pots and pans on the counters and on the old-fashioned stove in the corner. The pantry was always open and fully stocked with supplies. The door to the garden was usually open and a warm breeze filled the room. In the middle of the room sat a round wooden kitchen table with rush-bottomed chairs. And the kitchen was filled with something else—prayer.

Alice was one of the most prayerful people I've ever known. I could almost touch with my hand the prayers that flowed around that room. Prayers for me, prayers for family and friends, prayers for people who weren't very nice, prayers for the country and the world—all kinds of prayers, spoken and unspoken, made Alice and Fred's kitchen come alive. It was an experience I have never had in any church. I used to go over to their house, worried out of my mind, and they would immediately welcome me into their kitchen. I'd pull up a chair and share a cup of tea. I was always treated exactly like a member of their family: I was somebody special and at the same time nobody special at all.

Each time I entered Alice and Fred's kitchen was like a homecoming to me. When I crossed the threshold, the anxiety stopped at the kitchen door.

Get As Good As You Give

On one occasion when Jesus was going to the house of a leader of the Pharisees to eat a meal on the sabbath, they were watching him closely. . . . When [Jesus] noticed how the guests chose the places of honor, he told them a parable. "When you are invited by someone to a wedding banquet, do not sit down at the place of honor, in case someone more distinguished than you has been invited by your host; and the host who invited both of you may come and say to you, 'Give this person your place,' and then in disgrace you would start to take the lowest place. But when you are invited, go and sit down at the lowest place, so that when your host comes, he may say to you, 'Friend, move up higher'; then you will be honored in the presence of all who sit at the table

with you. For all who exalt themselves will be humbled,
and those who humble themselves will be exalted."

Luke 14:1; 7–11

Living hospitably includes the art of receiving hospitality graciously and humbly. Anxious types like me simply can't be choosy about where, when, or from whom to accept hospitality. Remember, no act of kindness is too small when anxiety threatens to pull us under for the third time. We respond to any hospitality offered us with grace and humility.

What I find so interesting about the parable of the wedding banquet is that Jesus is speaking to each of us. The piece reads a lot like advice from a first-century Miss Manners. Jesus observes the other dinner guests vying for the best seats at the table. (I've always imagined the scene as a type of musical chairs, with lots of pushing and straining for the remaining dinner chairs.) Knowing "they were watching him closely," Jesus recommends they might try humbly accepting hospitality so that honor may be conferred by the host—a somewhat oblique reference that God may in fact be the real host at dinner.

In the verses that follow, Jesus goes on to advise the dinner guests to offer hospitality to the unworthy: "Go out at once into the streets and lanes of the town and bring in the poor, the crippled, the blind, and the lame" (Luke 14:21). All those sick and anxious people couldn't possibly offer hospitality in return. Then Jesus follows up his advice with a parable about a host who threw a dinner party for his friends, and no one bothered to come. (I thought they all gave *excellent* excuses for not being able to accept.) The host then invited the poor, the crippled, the blind, and the lame, and even compelled strangers to attend. The parable concludes with the host declaring that none who were initially invited to the banquet will ever taste his dinner.

In this parable it is now clear that God is indeed the Host who extends hospitality, which is really grace. And we find ourselves among those who graciously decline God's hospitality as well as the sick, anxious, unworthy ones who accept. When anxious people like us accept gracious offers of hospitality graciously, we give up control for a while. We cannot control the venue, the menu, or the retinue. It's simply not our party. We are at the mercy, if you will, of our Host. Every time we accept hospitality with grace and humility we practice the art of receiving God's grace into our anxious lives.

It's been an anxious day at work. An unexpectedly low quarterly earnings report, a semi-threatening statement to employees from the chief executive officer, and rumors of reorganization and lay-offs have exhausted my spirits. Wearily, I unlock the locks to the front security door and turn off the alarm. I'm surprised by a delicious smell coming from the kitchen. Alarmed, I tiptoe through the living room and dining room and peer through the kitchen door. No one is there. A pot of homemade beef stew simmers on the stove.

A fresh-baked loaf of bread sits on the counter, still warm from the oven. There's chocolate cake in the glass cake stand that wasn't there this morning. I quickly check the bedroom, bathroom, and study. No one. Returning to the kitchen, I notice a candle burning on the small table in the breakfast room. Warmed by the kitchen, the little room glows with candlelight. The table is set for one. A small glass of red wine is already poured. There are flowers. Suddenly the candle flickers and sputters, and I hear the soft beat of wings. It's good to be home again.

CHAPTER 4

the Garden:
Creativity

> *[Jesus] said to his disciples . . . "Consider the lilies,*
> *how they grow: they neither toil nor spin; yet I tell you,*
> *even Solomon in all his glory was not clothed like one of*
> *these. But if God so clothes the grass of the field, which*
> *is alive today and tomorrow is thrown into the oven,*
> *how much more will he clothe you—you of little faith!*
> *And do not keep striving for what you are to eat and*
> *what you are to drink, and do not keep worrying. For it*
> *is the nations of the world that strive after all these*
> *things, and your Father knows that you need them. In-*
> *stead, strive for his kingdom, and these things will be*
> *given to you as well.*   Luke 12:22a; 27–31

It is clear to me now that Jesus never had a mortgage. Lucky man. Mortgages are a necessary evil to modern society. It's interesting that the word "mortgage" contains *mort*, the French word for death. It sometimes seems as though my mortgage is suspended above my head like the sword of

Damocles. I now spend much of my waking life striving to pay the mortgage. And like most of us during these uncertain economic times, I worry about losing my job—and my house—and that I'll end up living in my 1986 standard Honda Civic hatchback.

Even if Jesus had overlooked a field of subdivisions, condominiums, or urban neighborhoods, he would most likely have eyes only for the grass and the lilies of the field. Life is filled with striving to survive—to put food on the table, to keep a home in which to shelter, to get a little security, to insure a better life for the kids. In this regard, life at the end of the twentieth century is no different than life at the beginning of the first century. It comes as no surprise that such striving creates a good deal of anxiety. If ever there was a generation that needed to consider the lilies of the field and God's providence, it's ours.

In Luke 12, Jesus turns our attention toward creation. Solomon in all his glory couldn't hold a candle to a single lily. Even the grass of the field shows forth the glory of God in his providence for and lordship over all creation. That's why God created gardens.

A garden soothes troubled hearts, delights the senses, feeds the body, and offers us a second Eden in which to play and rest. In the Bible gardens were places of creation. The world was created in a garden. Biblical writers, including Isaiah, used gardens as places of healing and enjoyment. Isaiah 58:11 promises healing and transformation to God's people when they behave justly toward their neighbors in need. And out of the desolation and devastation of a sun-scorched land the Lord will heal and strengthen the people, making them a well-watered garden, a source of life and nourishment to all who need them. Out of all of our pain and sorrow God creates in us a living garden of hope and healing. In the hands of the Lord our pain is transformed into a thing of beauty. Amidst all our anxious striving with mortgages, kids, jobs, and life in general, God leads us to a garden—and shows us a lily.

Gardens are creative places. When we create and maintain a garden, we create a place where we can walk with our Creator in the cool of the day. The garden is the place where we discover faith is a work of art.

At least that's what I told myself when I decided to plant the front and back gardens of my new house. When I moved in, the front yard contained dead grass in soil the consistency of asphalt, lots of tree roots from the liquid amber on the other side of the broken sidewalk, and three camellia trees. The back yard was worse. It was paved badly with pieces of old, broken sidewalk and concrete. A rotten porch roof and fence defined the back of the property. Needless to say, everything else in the back yard was rotten too—except for a small, ragged orange tree, an overgrown camellia bush, an anemic lemon tree, and a huge fica tree the size of a three-story house.

Of course, I responded to the decay in my "gardens" in

typical fashion. When I came home from work I would shut my eyes until I could get my key in the front door. I only went out back to take out the garbage. And all the while I worried and stewed about how I could possibly create gardens out of what clearly were wastelands. Luckily, I had enough mental health left to ask for help. I called a professional landscaper.

I took a week's vacation to assist Cecily the landscaper prepare and plant the front garden. In just three days the two of us moved five tons of old roots, dead grass, topsoil, compost, and mulch. As Cecily took the first ton of material to the dump, I took a well-earned break. Although it was only February, the California sky was cloudless and the temperature a perfect 70 degrees. I sat down to rest on the newly-turned earth with my back propped against the foundation of the house. I was pleasantly exhausted with that good kind of tired that comes from doing manual labor for a whole day, knowing all the while I would soon return to a comfortable desk job. The soil was now soft and comfortable to sit on. I closed my eyes and felt the warm sun on my face. Having survived sixty-seven years of earthquake, storm and sun, my new old house felt strong and cool against my back. Unexpectedly, I had an over-powering feeling of well being. I thought, *This is really a good thing.* For the very first time I felt like a homeowner—not in a possessive sense, but that this home was an incredible gift from God to me. The house was mine because God gave it to me. And it was very good.

Moving seven tons of soil and rock is hard work. That in itself was not creative. But I learned there could be no garden, no creation, without the hard work needed to prepare for planting. I put my own sweat and toil into making my garden; in fact, I put a lot of myself into it. And as I sat on the ground and leaned against my house, I slowly began to wonder if this is how God felt at the end of each day of creation.

God had a lot of hard work to do before he put in the garden of Eden. How did I ever get the idea that creating the universe, or any other miraculous act for that matter, is easy for God? How in heaven's name would I know? But after spending seven days working in my own garden, I began to believe that God must have sweated and toiled over Eden. In other words, he must have put something of himself into his creation. And God must have thoroughly enjoyed it.

Dorothy Sayers once wrote that we are most like God when we create.[1] She meant that when we create something, like a garden, a poem, a needlepoint project, or a rocking chair, we most clearly reflect the image of God in us. When we let ourselves be creative, the Spirit of God and our humanity work together to create beauty. We don't have to be talented to be creative. Of course, its wonderful to be talented at playing the violin or painting landscapes. However, the ability to create goes way beyond talent. Our Creator made each of us to be creative beings. That need to create is internal; it's the way we're put together, regardless of talent.

Living a creative life has far more to do with being faithful, not talented. I recently read about a woman entrepreneur who, in middle age, learned to hand paint porcelain cups, saucers, and teapots. She commented, "When I saw my first hand-painted china, I knew that's what I wanted to do with my life."[2] On her paper-thin creations she paints delicate flowers and vines. She sells her porcelain creations to boutiques and specialty shops. When the interviewer asked what advice she might give others interested in her craft, she said, "Paint every day whether you feel like it or not." She lives creatively because she is faithful to her craft.

Christians are called not only to be faithful to our creative passion, art, or craft, but to be faithful to God. Living a creative life is living a faithful life. When we live our passion to create teacups or gardens, God invites us to bring that same creative passion to life with him, a life that never ends. To live creatively, we blend skill with imagination: we bring whatever hard-won skills or discipline we have to create whatever it is we see in the twinkle of our mind's eye. And when everything starts to come together, when skill serves the imagination and the "artwork" begins to take shape, we become "enthused," which in Greek literally means "to be in God." Through the door of our creative effort we enter that deep place in us where God's Spirit lives, where faith begins, and we are satisfied, content, at peace.

As I was agonizing about whether to buy my house, a well-meaning friend said to me, "Look. A house is just shelter. Nothing more. That's how you have to think about it." Others have since espoused this real estate philosophy. I find such philosophy sadly lacking. While I do need shelter to survive, I am not simply an animal looking for a convenient cave. As a human being, I bring to the purchase of a house a complex web of dreams, emotions, life experiences, and childhood memories that form my heart's understanding of *home*. Buying a home is as much a matter of the heart as the head.

My home is a living, creative work in process. Homemaking, which in my view includes gardening, is a creative effort. It is much more than dusting once a week, cleaning the bathroom, or cooking dinner. Nor is it weeding, watering, or fertilizing. Homemaking is the art of making a home out of a house and a garden out of a wasteland. Homemaking is like writing, designing jewelry, or playing the violin. It takes skill, diligence, practice, and an occasional willingness to try something new. Homemaking is a form of self-expression. Homemaking and gardening creatively express those unique dreams, emotions, and memories each of us has inside us about *home*. And about Christ, our heart's true home.

When I began to write seriously, my head was filled with fanciful notions about the romantic lives writers lead. I imagined writers glorying in the solitary life, living quietly, but intensely, in the gentle New England countryside or on the wild, ravaging Pacific coast. I imagined them awakening each morning, after an evening of deep self-reflection in front of the fire, to record profound and beautiful thoughts in little, elegant journals. Of course, they enjoyed relationships with interesting, slightly bohemian people who engaged them in witty conversations and intelligent discussions. I imagined Christian writers living in much the same way, only that God gave them a succession of life-changing spiritual experiences.

I've since learned that writers are ordinary, anxious people with families to support, who, after the kids are in bed, spend a lot of time at the kitchen table or in the basement writing as though their lives depended on it. Living the creative life, I've discovered, isn't necessarily romantic. Living creatively requires great stick-to-it-ness, the willingness to be faithful no matter what. Living a creative and faithful life requires hard work, discipline, and skill motivated by imagination and love.

Let me go back to moving all those rocks. Did I mention that I moved two tons, one rock at a time? My love of gardening kept me going. I would carry a stone from the rock pile and give it to Cecily, who would carefully build a rock wall to create a terrace for the garden. I had to work slowly to avoid injury to my back or to prevent dropping a stone on my toes. I learned that creating a garden is very hard work. Each time I lifted a rock, I kept imagining a beautiful garden with a rock wall. The hard, physical labor of moving a rock pile was an unexpected antidote to anxiety—after all, how could I worry and fret while busy moving stones? My world shrank from one of boundless, unending, nightmarish scenarios, feeding on my already anxious mind, to me, Jesus, and the rock in my hands, carried one step at a time.

Faithfully moving those rocks helped a garden come alive that had previously only been a dream. Five months later, I had a lush front garden in hues of blue, lavender, purple, white, pale yellow, and pink. In my fifteen-by-ten-foot plot I now grow the following: three kinds of lavender, two creeping roses, flowering catnip, rosemary, a variety of sage and penstemon, two bushes of artemisia, golden poppies, lobelia, alyssum, candytufts, quince, a variety of salvia, a broom plant, a bougainvillea, a strange kind of purple geranium, and, right in the middle of the garden, a flowering tree.

Sow What?

"A sower went out to sow his seed; and as he sowed, some fell on the path and was trampled on, and the birds of the air ate it up. Some fell on the rock; and as it grew up, it withered for lack of moisture. Some fell among thorns, and the thorns grew with it and choked

> *it. Some fell into good soil, and when it grew, it pro-*
> *duced a hundredfold." As he said this, he called out,*
> *"Let anyone with ears to hear listen!"*   Luke 8:5–8

It's easy for me to forget the sower when I read this parable. I usually jump right into the part about rocks, thorns, and good soil, and worry that I'm all rocks and thorns and that any good soil I might have once had has now eroded. But Jesus' parable begins with the sower. "A sower went out to sow his seed" reminds me of the opening verse in John's gospel: "In the beginning was the Word, and the Word was with God, and the Word was God" (John 1:1). Both passages ultimately have roots in Genesis. "In the beginning when God created the heavens and the earth" (Gen. 1:1). The sower is the Creator whose seed is the spoken, life-giving Word. In fact, the sower as Creator and Word Spoken is reinforced by the signature of Jesus' parable, "Let anyone who has ears to hear listen!"—God enters our hearts through our ears.

Jesus tells us to *listen*. Living the creative life is founded on listening. Musicians and composers must listen to create their art. Artists listen to their inner muse to discover the form their art must take. Strong marriages and lasting friendships are founded on and sustained by listening to one another. Because the spiritual life is also a form of the creative life, listening to God is essential.

Jesus chooses a garden in which to cast his parable. The sower is the Creator; Jesus' listeners are different kinds of soil; the seed is the word of God. What God creates is a living relationship with us through his word. Of course, how well we listen to God's word helps shape the quality of life with God. The good soil, Jesus' listeners in whom his word is firmly planted, produces a hundred-fold. Like growing a garden, our relationship with the Creator is living and growing, a creative act that cultivates life and beauty.

God sows the word in us, making a relationship with him possible. But Jesus warns us about those things that would distract us from creating a life with him. I am particularly sensitive to Jesus' admonition about thorns—the cares of the world (i.e., all that anxiety and worry over how I'm to support the solidly middle-class lifestyle to which I've become accustomed). Any gardener knows it's far easier to grow thorns and weeds than flowers and food. The prickly thorns of anxiety too often hinder me from living creatively with God.

God calls us to live with him in other creative ways, to prepare the soil of our hearts with ears well-tuned to his word. There are countless ways in which to live creatively with God. Any work, art or craft for which God gives us a special passion, any way in which we feel compelled to create life, beauty and hope, is living creatively with God. Homemaking, gardening, and writing are my passions. I don't necessarily have a natural talent for any of these, but I do have a sincere love for such activities that open me to the quiet, mysterious movements of God. When I am gardening, I am like the man Paul wrote about in 2 Corinthians 12:2, who was mysteriously "caught up to the third heaven." Time slips away. I no longer worry and my mind quiets and clears.

Due to Forces Beyond Our Control

Then he told this parable: "A man had a fig tree planted in his vineyard; and he came looking for fruit on it and found none. So he said to the gardener, 'See here! For three years I have come looking for fruit on this fig tree, and still I find none. Cut it down! Why should it be wasting the soil?' He replied, 'Sir, let it alone for one more year, until I dig around it and put manure on it. If it bears fruit next year, well and good; but if not, you can cut it down.'"   Luke 13:6–9

Good gardeners can be merciless. My former landlord, Al, is a master gardener. It seems to me he knows everything about plants and how they grow. Al has a green thumb in spades. His two-acre estate is rich with flowers, shrubs, fruit trees, herbs, and even a vineyard. He loves his various gardens and spends most of his spare time gardening. While Al may love the plants he grows, he has no romantic or sentimental ideas about gardening. If a plant fails to produce or no longer fits in the landscape design, he ruthlessly pulls it out or cuts it down to make way for more productive or more attractive plants.

In Jesus' parable of the fig tree, the gardener's response to the landlord surprises me. When the landlord tells him to cut down the barren fig tree, the gardener argues for mercy on behalf of the tree and promises to give it special attention. "Sir, let it alone for one more year, until I dig around it and put manure on it." But even the gardener has limits to his mercy—"If it bears fruit next year, well and good; but if not, you can cut it down."

I heard recently on the radio a quote by Edwin Land, inventor of the Polaroid Land camera: "Central to creativity is the willingness to fail." To be creative and try something new in our art, craft, or spiritual life is worth the risk of failure. It's "pushing the envelope"—that willingness to experiment to grow and produce something new and different. The gardener is willing to risk saving the tree from the landlord by taking a different approach to cultivating it.

Jesus doesn't tell us whether he succeeds in growing a more productive tree. The scary part of living a creative life, especially a creative spiritual life, is the possibility of failure, of getting the technique wrong or ruining the painting or using clumsy words in prayer. The scary part is we are not in control of our creative impulses. God is.

And that's the difference between creating a spiritual life and practicing an art or craft. Because God is the source of our creativity we cannot fail. The spiritual life isn't about technique or finished product; the spiritual life is about letting God the Creator, in whose hands are mercy and grace, work through us in every area of our lives.

We don't make a garden; God makes the garden. Paul knew it when he wrote, "I planted, Apollos watered, but God gave the growth" (1 Cor. 3:6). The gardener in Jesus' parable knew the tree might have to be cut down, but he was willing to try something new to save it.

Jesus isn't interested in business as usual. Jesus is interested in creating with us an ever-new relationship with God. Jesus is interested in whether we are willing to be creative in our spiritual lives, whether we are willing to risk seeming failure. Jesus calls each of us to push the envelope with him, all the while assuring us that in him we cannot fail. Are we, like the gardener, willing to step out into the unknown trusting that God the Creator is at work?

We begin with faith as small as a mustard seed. Living a creative spiritual life begins with paying attention to the small ordinary people and events in our lives. We focus on the minutia in which is hidden the kingdom of God. In her book *Bird By Bird: Some Instructions on Writing and Life*, Anne Lamott advises writers to write short assignments.[3] Anyone who sits down to write the great American novel in an afternoon probably won't produce very much. Rather, Lamott recommends, write enough words every day to fill up a one-inch by one-inch picture frame. Such a picture frame sits on Lamott's desk, and she writes enough words (often more than enough) to fill it up every day. The writing doesn't have to be perfect or even very good. The secret to creative writing comes by writing faithfully—every day, word by word.

The secret to living a creative spiritual life is to consider the lilies of the field—faithfully listening to God create his Spirit anew in us and in our world.

Spring is on its way in my garden. The garden has that tired winter look. Most plants have not yet begun to flower, and bulbs are just beginning to push up earth. The winter rains left plenty of large weeds behind. Under a clear, California-blue sky, I kneel and pull one weed at a time, carefully feeling at the base of each weed so as to pull it out by the roots. Grab, feel, pull. Grab, feel, pull. Just me, weeds, and sky.

I grab another weed and feel for the roots. A tingling sensation shoots up my right arm. I let go the weed and rub my hand. The earth begins to shake slightly; then there's a sound like a speeding freight train. Suddenly a large tree shoots up from the ground where the weed once was. Knocked on my back by the force of the tree, I look up into its branches. Stars hang on every limb. Its leaves stream light. I see darkness in between its branches, and glory shimmers there. And in my hand is a small, fragrant lily.

CHAPTER 5

the Bedroom:
Prayer

[Jesus] entered a certain village, where a woman named Martha welcomed him into her home. She had a sister named Mary, who sat at the Lord's feet and listened to what he was saying. But Martha was distracted by her many tasks; so she came to him and asked, "Lord, do you not care that my sister has left me to do all the work by myself? Tell her then to help me." But the Lord answered her, "Martha, Martha, you are worried and distracted by many things; there is need of only one thing. Mary has chosen the better part, which will not be taken away from her."

He was praying in a certain place, and after he had finished, one of his disciples said to him, "Lord, teach us to pray, as John taught his disciples." He said to them, "When you pray, say:

Father, hallowed be your name.

    Your kingdom come.

    Give us each day our daily bread.

    And forgive us our sins,

for we ourselves forgive everyone indebted to us.
And do not bring us to the time of trial."

Luke 10:38–11:4

I couldn't sleep that first night in my new house. As the house settled on its sixty-seven-year-old frame, it creaked and groaned. I kept hearing the water heater turn on and off. An unfamiliar dog barked frantically outside. And what was that sound at the window? Around one o'clock in the morning I actually convinced myself that some inner-city gang had surrounded my house and was about to break down the doors using heavy, steel-toed boots. I tossed and turned, tossed and turned. At about three o'clock, I began to pray, "Oh God, what have I done? Buying this house was a terrible mistake. Please get me out of here! Amen."

I believe our most honest, heartfelt prayers are the ones we pray in the middle of the night. Those prayers may not be very brave or noble or holy, but they come straight from the heart to God's ear. Lying in bed late at night with exhausted bodies and anxious minds, our usual, daily social defenses are all that's asleep. We are most open to God our Creator who knows our innermost thoughts, our most secret dreams. In the middle of the night, when we can't get off that anxious treadmill of worry and fear, the words "Please God, help!" form on our lips, take wing, and fly through the darkness.

Martha is a terrific Christian. She does everything right. She welcomes Jesus into her home and offers him hospitality to make him comfortable. With not much help in the kitchen, who can blame her if she gets just a teeny-weenie bit frazzled? Meanwhile, Martha's sister Mary sits all dreamy-eyed, resting at Jesus' feet, doing nothing but hanging on his every word. Jesus seems to be enjoying himself immensely. So Martha takes a small shot at Mary through Jesus: "Lord, do you not care that my sister has left me to do all the work by myself? Tell her then to help me."

Lord, do you not *care*. . . . Martha's shot hits the bull's eye, and Jesus feels the sting of her words. With boundless tenderness, he looks straight into Martha's anxious heart. After a long silence, Jesus almost whispers, "Martha, Martha, you are worried and distracted by many things; there is need of only one thing. Mary has chosen the better part, which will not be taken away from her."

"There is need of only one thing." Anxiety is fueled by the need to do (or feel) everything at once for everybody until our lives are so complicated we no longer enjoy the presence of God in our homes. The simplicity "of only one thing" soothes our anxious hearts with the simple presence of Jesus. And so we come to the heart of the spiritual life—resting in God through prayer.

Learning What Comes Naturally

A firefighter in Oklahoma City appears on the television and is shown carrying the lifeless body of a child. Two Americans are released into the bright Iraqi sunlight after four month's imprisonment. On trial for drowning her two small sons, a young mother sobs before a southern jury. In a cosmic *pas de deux*, an American space shuttle docks with a Russian space station for the first time in history. In each case, our first response is to pray. We human beings are built for prayer. From "O dear God" when shocked by tragedy to "Thank you, God" during an unexpected triumph, prayer leaps to our lips from the core of our being.

"Teach us to pray" has echoed down the ages as humanity's most heartfelt plea. For untold centuries we humans have sought to pray. In fact, the desire and ability to pray is one of the characteristics that sets us apart from the animal world. While there is much humans share with the animal kingdom, the art of prayer is unique to humanity. Many scientists have shown that whales speak a kind of language. Some primates have been trained to speak American Sign Language. Dolphins display an intelligence startlingly similar to humans. Some birds even have the ability to use tools, a trait formerly believed to be exclusively human. However, prayer is one of the great faculties we humans have in common only with other human beings. The desire and ability to pray transcends race, gender, culture, class, nations, and even time itself.

Essentially, the great religions of the world chart the human quest for when and how, and to whom, to pray.

In Luke's gospel, the giving of the Lord's Prayer follows immediately after Jesus' visit to Martha's home. Jesus is praying in a certain place when an un-named disciple asks to learn how to pray, a request as ancient as time and filled with human longing. I like to think of that unknown disciple as being Martha, who has come in search of Jesus so that she may learn the need of only one thing. In Luke's gospel, Jesus answers her with one simple prayer:

> Father, hallowed be your name.
>> Your kingdom come.
>> Give us each day our daily bread.
>> And forgive us our sins,
>>> for we forgive everyone indebted to us.
>> And do not bring us to the time of trial.

In Matthew's gospel, Jesus delivers the Lord's Prayer in the context of a broader teaching against hypocrisy and our human obsession to "see and be seen." Jesus warns against "practicing your piety before others in order to be seen by them" (Matt. 6:1). He then prefaces the Lord's Prayer with "whenever you pray, go into your room and shut the door and pray to your Father who is in secret" (Matt. 6:6). The issue here is power: who's got a direct line to God and who doesn't.

Sometimes public prayer can be used to demonstrate who is holier than someone else. Probably all of us, at one time or another, have been lectured to or preached at by someone praying aloud in a public prayer gathering. I myself have been known to rise to the prayerful occasion, dazzling the faithful with elocution matched only by the eloquence of my words. In Matthew, Jesus offers the Lord's Prayer as a private prayer, an antidote to long-winded public prayers that too often focus more on the one who prays than the One for whom prayers are intended.

And so we go into our room, shut the door, and come before Jesus with the same ancient longing as Martha—to discover the need of only one thing, a life lived for God alone. "Lord, teach us to pray." With the simplicity of the Lord's Prayer offered by Luke in combination with Matthew's admonishment to "shut the door and pray," we discover the essence of private prayer. While the Lord's Prayer certainly has a place in public worship or anywhere two or three are gathered in Jesus' name, we'll focus exclusively on private prayer as a way to combat anxiety.

I use the phrase "private prayer" deliberately. Private prayer may include personal prayers—those prayers about people and situations that have an impact on us personally. Personal prayers also have a place in public prayer. But private prayer is, well, *private*. It requires we retreat for a time to the privacy of the soul's innermost sanctum. And there, in the solitude of each heart, we sit at Jesus' feet and rest in God.

When I was still renting a cottage in the Oakland hills, the bedroom in my home had no door, and, worse yet, guests had to troop through the bedroom to get to the bathroom. Though I kept the bedroom scrupulously clean and tidy, I was always slightly uncomfortable with people using it as a hallway to the bathroom. I felt as though my privacy had been invaded somehow. When I bought my new house I was delighted to have a bedroom with a door and a bathroom with its own entrance.

The bedroom walls are painted a very pale blue; the ceiling and art deco molding around the windows and closets are bright white. The bed is piled high with a featherbed, feather comforters and pillows—all in white linen. Because the bedroom gets very hot in the summer, I installed a ceiling fan over the bed. The antique nightstand contains the book I'm currently reading, a flashlight, and a few personal items. An antique rosewood bureau stands against one wall; a quilt rack my father built for me decorates the other wall. The overall feel of the room is crisp, cool, restful, and private. When Jesus said, "go into your room and shut the door and pray" I think of my bedroom because it is my private sanctuary for prayer.

The bedroom is a place of rest. Resting is important to God. After creating the universe, God rested on the seventh day. Resting is so important that God calls his people to regular times of rest. On the Sabbath the people of God rest completely to express their complete trust in the Lord of all creation. During the Sabbath all work is put away; all eyes rest only on the Lord God.

Prayer is Sabbath. No matter what the actual content of our prayers, in prayer God calls us to trust him, to rest in him. When we pray, we lay down our burdens before the throne of Grace. Whether we pray for ourselves or others, we put ourselves or those for whom we pray to rest in God's hands. When we go into the bedroom and shut the door, we enter the Sabbath.

Resting in God is what trusting in God feels like. I once read a book by a Christian author which denounced "bosom-flyers," people who fly to rest on Jesus' bosom at the least sign of trouble in their lives. Well, I hope I *am* a bosom-flyer. For one thing, anxiety is exhausting. We anxious people need as much rest as we can get. And anxious people like me need to have a regular time of giving up control of the universe to God. We are in need of only one thing. We need the Sabbath. We need to go into our room and shut the door. Once there, we need to fly to Jesus' bosom and rest in his graceful arms.

Julian of Norwich

Julian of Norwich was a fourteenth-century Christian mystic, who, like Mary, sought to rest at Jesus' feet in pursuit of "only one thing." She *literally* went into her room, shut the door, and never came out.

In early Christianity "anchorites" were people who went to live in secluded, desert places where they could be free to pray without distraction. The word *anchorite* has its roots in a Greek verb that means "to retire." Of course, *retire* has two meanings—to retreat and to rest. Christian mystics often retired from everyday life to live with God alone.

Julian of Norwich was an anchoress. By the fourteenth century, many anchorites no longer withdrew to the desert; instead, they remained in busy cities and towns, but secluded themselves in cells or rooms built on the sides of churches, much like barnacles on the hull of a ship. Carol Flinders writes that "the ceremony of enclosure," a ceremony in which the anchorite was actually sealed inside his or her cell, was basically a burial service at which the last rites were given. The newly enclosed anchorite voluntarily committed him- or herself to remain there until death. Flinders observes, "The purpose of anchoritic enclosure was no heroic asceticism, however, but rather a complete openness to God in prayer."[1]

The word *cell* brings to our modern minds all sorts of images of imprisonment, discomfort, and loneliness. But Julian's cell was more like a small house. According to writings of the age, it most likely contained one large room, including a room specifically devoted to prayer. There was a small window that opened out onto the world where people could come to seek Julian's advice on spiritual matters. Another small window was cut into the wall of the church so Julian could take part in worship services, as well as partake of the Lord's Supper. Julian had a maid, Alice, who cooked and cleaned for her. She most likely also had a cat to catch the legion of mice inhabiting a seaport town such as Norwich. Part of Julian's enclosure probably included access to the church courtyard or garden, in which she could stroll.

Carol Flinders observes, "We might still shudder at the whole idea of such radical enclosure, but we must bear in mind, too, that the gifted artist in any medium requires a measure of silence and privacy, and the man or woman with a bent for contemplative prayer—a genius for inwardness itself—is no exception."[2] Julian sought to rest in God by living only with God in prayer and adoration. Her "retirement" was filled by conversation with God, filled with experiences of Christ's great suffering and the Spirit's boundless joy—especially joy. In her own book, Julian's message from God to the anxious world is to rest in God and "all shall be well, and every kind of thing shall be well."[3]

Needless to say, living the life of an anchorite is not possible, nor desirable, for most Christians today. And many of us may not have the gift of pure contemplation, that "genius for inwardness itself." Yet Jesus calls each of us to seek him in private prayer and rest in God.

The Dark Night of the Soul

However, resting in God isn't necessarily restful. We don't easily lay down our burdens before God's throne.

Paradoxically, entering the Sabbath in prayer is work. Anybody who has seriously pursued a life of prayer, especially private prayer, eventually experiences what many call "the dark night of the soul." Sometimes this experience is compared to a spiritual desert. The dark night of the soul may fall because we are anxious over someone or something in our lives; or it may come as a result of nothing at all. A time of extreme spiritual darkness and aridity, it happens to the most faithful Christians. The dark night of the soul is essentially a mystery that seems to happen *because* we are faithful disciples of Jesus Christ. It is because we are faithful that our prayers go out into a desert night to wander unanswered. Even the comfort of God's presence seems to abandon us, and we feel alone in a dark, dry place. "Lord, do you not care?" we ask. However, it is during the dark night of the soul that we are called to rest in a God we can no longer see, we can no longer hear, we can no longer feel.

I know a man whose fifteen-year-old daughter, Susan, was addicted to drugs. When he found out about it, he was furious at having been betrayed by someone he loves and at the same time terrified for her; he also felt completely helpless—and was angry at God for not protecting his child. After spending many angry, anxious nights in prayer, he lay awake one particular night, pleading with God to save his daughter from the demonic clutches of drug addiction. He told me that after a long time of agonizing in prayer, there came a brief moment when he felt he and his daughter were in God's hands, no matter what the future held. He was still very worried about her, but for a little while he just lay there resting in the Lord.

After an evening Passover meal, Jesus goes out into the darkness to the Mount of Olives.

> *And the disciples followed him. When he reached the place, he said to them, "Pray that you may not come into the time of trial." Then he withdrew from them about a stone's throw, knelt down, and prayed, "Father, if you are willing, remove this cup from me; yet, not my will but yours be done." Then an angel from heaven appeared to him and gave him strength. In his anguish he prayed more earnestly, and his sweat became like great drops of blood falling down on the ground.* Luke 22:39b–44

The suffering that awaits Jesus in the morning begins on the Mount of Olives. Jesus prays a Sabbath prayer, a prayer to rest in the will of the Father. Nonetheless, it is a prayer prayed in excruciating agony, despite an angel's ministrations. His is the original dark night of the soul.

Long after Good Friday and long after Easter, Julian of Norwich speaks to us across the centuries. "Pray inwardly, even if you do not enjoy it. It does good, though you feel nothing. Yes, even though you think you are doing nothing."[4]

The Widow and the Rabbi

Then Jesus told them a parable about their need to pray always and not to lose heart. He said, "In a certain city there was a judge who neither feared God nor had respect for people. In that city there was a widow who kept coming to him and saying, 'Grant me justice against my opponent.' For a while he refused; but later he said to himself, 'Though I have no fear of God and no respect for anyone, yet because this widow keeps bothering me, I will grant her justice, so that she may not wear me out by continually coming.'" And the Lord said, "Listen to what the unjust judge says. And will not God grant justice to his chosen ones who cry to him day and night? Will he delay long in helping them? I tell you, he will quickly grant justice to them. And yet, when the Son of Man comes, will he find faith on earth?" Luke 18:1–8

Many years ago I got a call from the California Highway Patrol. Calmly and slowly the voice on the phone said, "Mr. Ronald Johnson has been killed in a freeway accident. I'm with his widow now, and she's hysterical. Would you come over and stay with her until we can contact relatives?" Jeanine and her husband, Ronald, were good friends of mine from church. It was a rainy day, about two o'clock in the afternoon, and Ron was dead. As I jumped in my car to drive the few blocks to the

Johnson's house, I fought back waves of nausea as the news began to sink in. "No time for grief now—later, later," I told myself desperately. "I have to keep calm for Jeanine."

When I arrived at the Johnson's, an officer answered the door and quickly ushered me into the living room. Jeanine was beyond tears; she was doubled over on the couch crying great, gasping, screaming sobs, the kind that would later leave her feeling hollow and empty. Her two children, aged ten and seven, were standing over her, terrified, trying to make her stop crying, knowing their dad was dead but not understanding it—yet. I walked over to Jeanine and held her in my arms. Fresh grief made her grip me hard. Jeanine buried her face in my hair and through her sobs pleaded with me to "Tell me he's with Jesus! Tell me he's with Jesus!" over and over. Of course, Jeanine was really demanding a response from God, not me. Nonetheless, I whispered in Jeanine's ear, "Ron's with Jesus. Yes, he's with Jesus," and prayed to God that it was true.

Like the widow in Jesus' parable, Jeanine demanded justice. She demanded God give her justice against death, her opponent. She demanded to know whether a horrible wrong would be set right, that her husband of twenty-five years would live again with God. I believe Jesus' parable of the widow and the unjust judge brings us to the deepest, most central Christian experience: to pray for justice, that the world be made right for us, our loved ones, our communities, and that we not lose heart.

How do we pray at 3:00 A.M. when God seems against us? Like the widow, we pray by demanding (crying, whining, or sobbing) over and over again that justice be done, that the righteous be restored, that the world be recreated as God intended in the Garden. "And will not God grant justice to his chosen ones who cry to him day and night? Will he delay long in helping them?"

Christian faith begins by believing in the gospel of Jesus Christ. At the very heart of his gospel Jesus assures us that God is just, that our twin opponents of darkness and death will be vanquished forever. "And yet when the Son of Man comes, will he find faith on earth?" The essence of Christian spiritual experience is to hang on to Jesus' gospel with all our might, to pray for justice and not lose heart in a world where bad things continually happen to good people—in spite of all our worrying and fretting. And what happens when, driven by an anxious frenzy, I do lose heart at 3:00 A.M, and, turning my back on God, I roll over in bed in search of rest that will not come? The Son of Man leans over the bedside, covering me with his mercy, holding me with his grace until morning finally comes.

In prayer, we are called to rest under the eye of a just, and merciful, God. Executing justice with mercy is how God shows his love for us. God loves us by setting horrible wrongs (the wrongs done to us and those we love and the wrongs we do others) to rights—if not now, then in the time to come.

Teach us to pray. Teach us to rest in the justice and mercy of God even when everything is so horribly, so desperately wrong, and the darkness wraps thickly around us. Jesus responds by praying the Lord's Prayer. In Luke's version, the theme of justice and mercy runs like a thread through this prayer.

The Lord's Prayer also teaches what we are to pray for. It is there we see what Jesus really wants from God—that justice and mercy be done. When we examine our own hearts, that same desire is at work in us and it is the fount from which all our deepest prayers spring. I'm not talking about praying for parking spaces or material wealth. I mean late at night, in the privacy of our hearts, what we really want from God is justice and mercy; for God to make everything all right again for ourselves, for those we love, and our communities.

Let's look at the Lord's Prayer again.

Father, hallowed be your name. We begin by honoring our Father.

Your kingdom come. We are to pray for God's kingdom in which we as God's ministers currently work to end all suffering and thwart the darkness of death by upholding the gospel's light. We are to pray for God's kingdom to reign finally on the earth, for justice to come swiftly and mercifully, putting all of God's creation to rights, so that the dead may live again in Christ.

Give us each day our daily bread. Hunger is death's companion. Justice happens whenever life triumphs over death. To ask God for our daily bread is to ask for justice, that out of God's mercy we be given what we need to survive and live with Christ today.

And forgive us our sins, for we ourselves forgive everyone indebted to us. A cry for forgiveness is a cry for justice—that the wrongs we inflict on the world be put to rights. And the cry for forgiveness is a cry for mercy—that in spite of whatever sins we have committed, we beg to rest in God's undying love for us. Having received mercy and pardon for our sins, we extend forgiveness to those who have wronged us.

And do not bring us to the time of trial. On the evening before his death, Jesus instructs his disciples to "Pray that you may not come into the time of trial" (Luke 22:40b). Like "forgive us our sins," praying to avoid the time of trial is a plea for mercy. It is a cosmic prayer, one that acknowledges the forces of good and evil at work in our lives. It is a prayer for justice. Though the forces of evil may tempt and try us, we pray evil will not triumph in the end.

Demand the Holy Spirit

So I say to you, Ask, and it will be given you;
search, and you will find; knock, and the door will be

> *opened for you. For everyone who asks receives, and ev-*
> *eryone who searches finds, and for everyone who knocks,*
> *the door will be opened. Is there anyone among you*
> *who, if your child asks for a fish, will give a snake in-*
> *stead of a fish? Or if the child asks for an egg, will give*
> *a scorpion? If you then, who are evil, know how to give*
> *good gifts to your children, how much more will the*
> *heavenly Father give the Holy Spirit to those who ask*
> *him!"* Luke 11:9–13

And so Jesus brings us to the Holy Spirit, the Comforter, the One who walks alongside. We are to pray for the Holy Spirit. After Jesus finishes reciting the Lord's Prayer, he immediately tells his disciples the parable of the friend who begs for three loaves of bread from a neighbor at midnight. His neighbor gives the loaves, not because of friendship, but because he wants to go back to bed. The parable is similar to the widow and the unjust judge. Then Jesus tells his disciples to be like the friend at midnight, like the widow in court. We are to be demanding.

Ask, seek, find. Jesus' words have all the urgency of a command. And before his disciples can wonder for what it is they are to ask, seek, and find, Jesus asks them a couple of questions about fatherhood. He asks, "If you then, who are evil, know how to give good gifts to your children, how much more will the heavenly Father give the Holy Spirit to those who ask him!" When we ask God to give us the gift of the

Holy Spirit, we pray that, through God's divine presence, all wrongs be mercifully put to rights. Jesus' exclamation is really a clincher to the Lord's Prayer. In fact, the Lord's Prayer is a prayer for the Holy Spirit.

Red Alert

"Be on guard so that your hearts are not weighed down with dissipation and drunkenness and the worries of this life, and that day catch you unexpectedly, like a trap. For it will come upon all who live on the face of the whole earth. Be alert at all times, praying that you may have the strength to escape all these things that will take place, and to stand before the Son of Man."
Luke 21: 34–36

My friend Liz is so strung out by anxiety, she claims that the only way she can get through each day is by praying. Now Liz has very unorthodox ideas about God. But she prays—all the time. God answers Liz's prayers, not because she is right, but because God loves her.

Jesus has special words for people like Liz and me. "Be on guard so that your hearts are not weighed down with dissipation and drunkenness and the worries of this life, and that day catch you unexpectedly, like a trap. . . . Be alert at all times, praying that you may have the strength to escape." I'd really hate to be so weighed down with worry that I miss a chance to see Jesus. There is so much more to life than worry and anxiety. Anxiety weakens us. It saps our strength. It diverts our attention from living and waiting for God. Like Liz, we need to pray as though our lives depended on it—because they do.

Teach us to pray. Teach us to live. Teach us to escape the worries of this world, to live and rest in You. The private prayers we pray at midnight are the prayers we live in the morning. Like the widow and the friend who comes at midnight, we demand justice and mercy of the Father day and night. We pray until our very lives become prayers.

There is no such thing as a spiritual wimp. To live is to pray and to pray is to live. It's that simple. Too often I persist in believing that prayer is some kind of magic formula—if I can just say the right words, all my worries will melt away, when in fact I already have all I need to pray. It's not that I don't know how to pray; I have the Lord's Prayer and the Holy Spirit. It's not that I don't have time to pray; I have twenty-four hours in the day, the same as everybody else. What makes prayer hard is coming under the eye of God and telling him what I need, and resting in a just and merciful God. What makes prayer hard is relinquishing control—giving up drunkenness, dissipation, or worry—long enough to let God do his job.

For anxious people, simplicity is the key. Whatever the content, our prayers should be simple. In prayer, we simply tell God what we need. When I bought my house I was overwhelmed by anxiety. I wanted to tell God what I needed, but the need to be rescued from the perils of homeownership seemed to be enormous. During that time, I discovered a few simple prayers for anxious people.

"Lord Jesus Christ, have mercy on me, a sinner." This is an ancient prayer from the Eastern Orthodox Church. Russian pilgrims on long, difficult journeys prayed these words repeatedly to beg for God's mercy and strength. I found the prayer helped me cut through all the worries about crime in my neighborhood, buying a house in a soft market, and the overwhelming responsibilities of homeownership . . . to help me tell God simply what I needed. Like the Russian pilgrims long ago, I prayed the prayer over and over again throughout the day. Praying this way helped me pray for what I needed— God's mercy—instead of what I wanted—to be rescued.

The purpose of the prayer is to rest in God who promises mercy to all sinners in Jesus Christ. Pray the prayer throughout the day or night. Many people simplify the prayer even further by simply repeating a word or phrase within the prayer. For example, "Lord," "mercy," "Jesus," "Lord Jesus Christ," or "have mercy on me." All of our anxiety and worries are distilled into these words which are offered up to God.

"Jesus is Lord." This is the earliest Christian confession. It was proclaimed by believers before baptism. It tells the world

how Christians live—under Jesus' lordship and no one else's. To confess "Jesus is Lord" is to renounce any other claim we may have to lordship over our lives. For anxious people, confessing that "Jesus is Lord" helps us give up control over our lives and the lives of others.

I frequently say a personalized form of this ancient confession: "Jesus is Lord over me, over my house, over my neighborhood, over Oakland, over the Bay Area, over California, over the United States, and over the world." I repeat the prayer throughout the day. It's a kind of childish prayer, really, but it helps me to let go of worry and anxiety and rest in Jesus' lordship alone.

"God, help me!" is a perfectly legitimate prayer. Many of the Psalms are simply cries for divine help. I pray "God, help me!" frequently at night when darkness is literally all around. As a chronically anxious person, I constantly need God's help to survive the night. Author Esther de Waal offers a more elegant version of the prayer: "O God, come to my aid. Perfect [complete] in me the work you have begun."[5] Anxious people fear we won't survive the darkness of our anxiety. De Waal's prayer asks God to continue to work through us no matter how anxious we feel.

During the daytime, I find this prayer particularly helpful when I am gardening or involved in other creative work. It keeps me from worrying about producing a perfectly finished product . . . to pray only that God finish the work he has begun in me—no matter how the new book or new flowerbed turns out.

A picture hangs in my study. It is a wood-block print of a Celtic woman, dressed in the clothes of centuries ago, who has paused in her sweeping to bend over and examine the floor by candlelight. It is the artist's rendition of Jesus' parable of the lost coin. Printed next to the picture are the words of Esther de Waal: "She has made the mundane the edge of glory." The early Christian Celts believed all of what is life-giving to be seamless; there was no distinction between sacred and secular. They had a prayer for every activity, day or night. In Celtic spirituality, ordinary life is suffused with the light of the glory of God. The picture reminds me that it simply takes prayer to catch a glimpse of the holy—and to rest in the glory of God.

Benediction

Do not worry about anything, but in everything by prayer and supplication with thanksgiving let your requests be made known to God. And the peace of God, which surpasses all understanding, will guard your hearts and your minds in Christ Jesus.

Philippians 4:6–7

It takes faith to pray for justice. It takes faith to wait for God's justice and mercy to triumph. It takes faith to survive the dark night of the soul. It takes faith to pray always and not lose heart. It takes faith to rest in the peace and glory of God.

That first sleepless night in my new house is finally past. The birds begin to sing before the sun rises, and, surprisingly, my heart lifts at their song. "We made it!" I say to the two cats curled up beside me. "We made it through the night in one piece! The house is still standing! We're going to be okay. Thank you, God!" And softly, a whisper in the early morning stillness, "Do not worry about anything, but in everything by prayer and supplication with thanksgiving let your requests be made known to God. And the peace of God, which surpasses all understanding, will guard your hearts and your minds in Christ Jesus." It's time to get dressed and go to work.

CHAPTER 6

the Study:
Study

"Be dressed for action and have your lamps lit; be like those who are waiting for their master to return from the wedding banquet, so that they may open the door for him as soon as he comes and knocks. Blessed are those slaves whom the master finds alert when he comes; truly I tell you, he will fasten his belt and have them sit down to eat, and he will come and serve them."

Luke 12:35–37

Though I like to refer to it grandly as "my study," it's really the spare bedroom. I spend most of my time in the study on weekends when the weather is too inclement for gardening. Located in the back of the house, it is a very pleasant, quiet room with three windows and lots of light. Shelves of books line the walls. My desk is by a window, which overlooks the back garden.

The walls of the study are painted a very light apricot color; the moldings around the windows and doors are white,

125

as is the ceiling. The window blinds are a dark green; the hardwood floor is stained and polished to a light oak color. Underneath the other two windows is a daybed. When guests aren't using it, the daybed is great for afternoon naps; every weekend I usually curl up there with a good book and two cats.

Until my house, I had always lived in one-bedroom apartments. My desk was usually awkwardly crammed in a corner of the bedroom and was never a pleasant place to spend long periods of time. I used to write in the living room or on the dining room table. Now that I have a study, it has become my favorite room in the house. To paraphrase Virginia Woolf, my study is truly a room of my own. It's such a luxury to have a whole room dedicated to reading, writing, study—and naps.

I use the word "study" very broadly to include Bible study, reading, journaling, writing, or simply thinking about whatever it is I'm currently studying. In this sense, I don't mean study as education, mastering facts and skills for use and application, although education may be a part of study. Study is holy play. I heard a quote from G. K. Chesterton who wrote, "Joy is the serious business of heaven." Study is serious joy, a time in which we can come to God with questions about life and faith, with the freedom, even, to offer God our doubts. Study goes beyond learning; study includes reflection, contemplation, a "mulling over" the life of faith. Study is a time in which we can seriously play with Scripture—not by taking Scripture lightly, but by study-ing Scripture under the grace and mercy of God with the freedom to ask the Lord sometimes tough, sometimes unan-swerable questions. Like Jacob at the foot of heaven's ladder, study is a time to wrestle with God—and be transformed.

"Blessed are those slaves whom the master finds alert when he comes; truly I tell you, he will fasten his belt and have them sit down to eat, and he will come and serve them." Study helps us stay alert to welcome the Master when he returns. Study is a way of paying attention to the work of God. Studying Scripture, as well as reading Christian and secular books, magazines, and newspapers, helps us to discern the movement of the Holy Spirit in our lives, in the lives of those we love, and in our communities and nation. When we study, we prepare ourselves for the Master's return. When we thoughtfully, playfully, and respectfully contemplate the Christian faith, Jesus himself serves us.

Study also focuses our anxious minds. Worry and vain imaginings change nothing in the anxious situations we may find ourselves. Study gives our minds and hearts something constructive to do and focuses us on "whatever is true, whatever is honorable, whatever is just, whatever is pure, whatever is pleasing, whatever is commendable, if there is any excellence and if there is anything worthy of praise, think about these things" (Phil. 4:8).

In this chapter, I will outline three different kinds of study to use in exploring the Christian spiritual life. The first is a kind of Bible study I learned many years ago at an Intervarsity Christian Fellowship retreat. The second is a way of reading the Bible with our hearts as well as our eyes. And finally, we'll look at reading novels as a way of studying Christian faith.

Searching for Clues

Many years ago I learned a new, exciting kind of Bible study during an Intervarsity Christian Fellowship retreat. Over the years since that time, I've simplified and modified the Bible study to help me channel anxious, nervous energy into something constructive.

This type of study is for those times when you really want to immerse yourself in study. It is like taking on a project for a while, and it works best using longer portions of Scripture, like chapters or whole books of the Bible. The point to studying the Bible in this way is to study the biblical text as though you are seeing it for the first time; you should try to set aside all of your assumptions and prior knowledge to let the Bible speak to you in fresh, sometimes surprising ways. As you study, you become the expert without relying on scholars or other Christian writers to tell you what the Bible means. In other words, you become like a detective searching for clues about what God may be saying to you through a portion of the Bible.

In preparation, you'll need to buy a large-print edition of

the Bible, which will be much easier to read than standard type. You will be highlighting and writing in this Bible, so find one you are comfortable marking up. You will also need a pencil and several text highlighters in many different colors.

An alternative, more labor-intensive way to prepare for this Bible study is to type out, double-spaced, a chapter or book of the Bible. If you have time, I recommend typing the selected chapter or book on the computer or typewriter. I have found that simply typing the text offers me quite a bit of insight into the chapter or book before I even begin the actual study. In fact, just typing a book or chapter of the Bible, and doing nothing more, can be a valuable study exercise in itself.

Once you have a large-print edition of the Bible or a hard copy of the chapter or book you are going to study, you are ready to begin. There are three questions to answer in this kind of Bible study:

1. What does it say?
2. What does it mean?
3. What does it mean to me?

These three questions form the three parts to the Bible study.

But first, remember to begin each time you study in prayer. Ask God to guide you by the Holy Spirit to keep your heart and mind open to whatever God is about to show you.

Part One: What Does It Say?

You will be reading several times through the chapter or book you've selected, each time using a different highlighter color to help you identify different clues in the text. As you read, choose one highlighter color for each of the following to help you see each clue. Highlight:

- Repeated words
- Repeated phrases
- Verb tense (present, past and future)
- Characters/speakers/audience or listeners
- Questions

- Commands
- Geographical settings
- References to time
- References to prophets/messiah/other biblical people
- Names for God

Also highlight:

- Anything else you see in the text that seems important to you

- Any clues that you've already highlighted elsewhere in the larger book or chapter

So, for example, let's take the passage Luke 12:35–40. By the end of your study, the passage will be very colorful. You can look back over the passage and discover the following clues you've highlighted in this section:

Pink highlights *repeated words*: comes, come, coming, will, house

Blue highlights *repeated phrases*: blessed are those

Green highlights *references to time*: waiting, hour, the middle of the night, near dawn, unexpected hour

Red highlights *characters*: master, slaves, owner of the house, thief, Son of Man

Yellow highlights *commands*: Be dressed for action and have your lamps lit, be like those, be ready

Purple highlights *references to other biblical people*: Son of Man

In the margin of the Bible or your hard copy, you can also make notes in pencil as questions and observations arise. These are observations only; you will make interpretations and applications of the text at the end of the study.

In Luke 12:35–40, your pencil notes tell you:

- The commands come at the beginning and the end of the parables.

- The section is in the future tense, except for the last verse, "the Son of Man *is* coming."

- Who is the Son of Man?

- See Luke 6:20–22 regarding "blessed." Is there a connection?

- Why does Jesus switch from telling about the master and the slaves to the homeowner and the thief?

- Where else does Luke use the word *knock*?

Part Two: What Does It Mean?

After you've finished highlighting and making notes, it's time to interpret the clues you've uncovered. You'll need to read the chapter or book one more time and answer as many of your questions as you can. Also, comment on your notes and explain them. As you read over everything you've done, ask yourself:

- What does it mean?

Record your answers, comments, and interpretations on clean paper, your computer, or your journal. You may wish to consult an atlas of the Bible to help you see geographical references, but try to avoid using commentaries. For now, *you* are the scholar and the authority on this particular chapter or book. Remember, you are the detective searching for clues about what God may be saying to you—not what some commentary is telling you God is saying.

Part Three: What Does It Mean to Me?

Finally, it's time to apply what you've learned. Once you've finished responding to your highlighting and notations, ask yourself:

- What new things has God shown me in my study?

- What is God saying to me, my church, or my community?

- What one thing does God want me to do as a result of my study?

Record your answers and thoughts. When you've finished, thank God for whatever he has revealed to you during the course of your study. Pray for the grace and strength to do what God is calling you to do.

Practicing "Holy Reading"

The next kind of study comes from an ancient Christian practice of reading the Bible, sometimes called by its Latin name, *Lectio Divina*. It means divine or "holy reading." I learned about holy reading from a wonderful book by Macrina Wiederkehr, *A Tree Full of Angels: Seeing the Holy in the Ordinary*.[1] The purpose of holy reading is to read slowly, thoughtfully, and prayerfully until we come quietly and silently to rest in God. The purpose of holy reading is not to gather information about God or his people, rather it is a way of reading the Bible *with* God, with his Spirit guiding and welcoming us as we read. Holy reading is a simple study tool to help us rest in Christ.

As anxious people, we often need simply to slow down and rest in God. Holy reading is a wonderful way to study and cope with anxiety. Holy reading can be used to read books in the Bible (in small pieces at a time over a period of time); to read whole stories in the Bible (for example, the story of Noah's ark); to read several verses (this works especially well with much of Leviticus, parts of Numbers and Deuteronomy, the Psalms, Ecclesiastes, and the Epistles).

As we explore the three different parts to holy reading, we'll use Luke 12:35-38 as our example.

Reading

The first step is choose which portion of the Bible you'd like to read. We've chosen Luke 12:35–38:

> *"Be dressed for action and have your lamps lit; be like those who are waiting for their master to return from the wedding banquet, so that they may open the door for him as soon as he comes and knocks. Blessed are those slaves whom the master finds alert when he comes; truly I tell you, he will fasten his belt and have them sit down to eat, and he will come and serve them. If he comes during the middle of the*

night, or near dawn, and finds them so, blessed are those slaves."

Begin by reading the passage very slowly. You are reading with God and he's in no hurry. You are not reading to gather information; your reading is being guided by God who wants to be with you and touch your heart through the Scriptures, rather than have you simply accumulate facts. Read your selection over and over, slowly, until you feel God touching you with a word, phrase, or story. For example, let's say you experienced God touching your heart with "open the door for him as soon as he comes and knocks."

Reflection and Prayer

The second step is to reflect and savor the portion of Scripture with which God has touched your heart. When you feel in your heart God touching you with a particular word, phrase, or story, stop reading. Take a deep breath, relax as much as you can, and let God speak to you through the Scriptures. Close your eyes and repeat the word or phrase over and over. Or, if God is using a story in the Bible to speak to you, imagine the scene, the characters, and the action. Take your time. Let the Scripture reach deep down into your heart. As you reflect on the passage, remain as open as you can to God guiding your thoughts and feelings. Don't be afraid to let God use your imagination to speak to you.

For example, as I reflect on "open the door for him as

soon as he comes and knocks," I begin to wonder what it feels like to open the door to the Master after a long, long time of waiting. Then I imagine waiting for the Master. How boring it is! I wait a very long time, and I grow worried the longer the delay. After a while, I begin to doubt whether he is coming at all. Then I begin to think I've been stood up! I get angry—after all, the house is clean and polished, tea is poured (which I took a great deal of trouble to prepare)—doesn't he care? There's nothing to do but wait.

I wait a very, very long time. I give up all hope of the Master's returning, and, suddenly, I'm very, very sleepy. I fall asleep on the couch. A long time passes. I hear a violent knock on my front door—*crack!* Startled, I try to get hold of myself and at the same time think, *He's here!* Terrified, I jump up, run to the door, and, gathering up all my courage, open it. Jesus is standing there with his hands on his hips, scowling. I can't move. His eyes begin to dissect me. I am way beyond fear now. The Master's examination seems to go on for centuries. Then the Master slowly begins to smile. *It's worth it!* I think. *It's worth all the waiting and fear and worry and anger!* As I welcome him in, I get a very strange but warm feeling that he is welcoming me.

After a while, you may feel God calling you to pray based on your time of reflection. By all means, pray! Pour out your heart. Tell God whatever it is he has shown you in your reflection time. It may be that God is moving you to pray the Lord's Prayer or one of the brief prayers mentioned in the last chapter. It may be that God is leading you to adoration and praise; or to tears; or to sing and dance; or to write or paint or garden in prayer; or to rest in him in silence. After reflecting on "open the door for him as soon as he comes and knocks," I pray, "Please let me feel welcome for a while. Comfort me with it. Please."

Contemplation

Prayer may lead you into contemplation. In holy reading, contemplation is not thinking about God. Contemplation is resting in God. Macrina Wiederkehr describes contemplation this way: "[In contemplation] we let go of our dependency on thoughts, words, and images. . . . We let the angels carry us. Surrender is the only word we know. . . . Nothing is left except being in God. . . . Contemplation is like going to heaven for a while."[2]

When I use holy reading as study, God sometimes leads me into contemplation, which for me is like a deep resting in God. In the example above, I rested in God; I surrendered my heart and my mind to God, and simply let God make me welcome for a little while.

Sometimes reading the Scriptures leads me into reflection and prayer, but not contemplation, and that's just fine. It's hard to know where prayer leaves off and contemplation begins. There is no clear distinction. The Christian spiritual life is not about identifying stages of various spiritual experiences. Remember, living the Christian spiritual life is an art, not a science. Remain in contemplation for as little or as long as you like.

The final kind of study I recommend is reading novels. As an anxious person, I have found that reading fiction helps me tremendously. Through novels I can enter another world or inhabit another's thoughts so I can see my own world better. Not only does fiction entertain me, but through stories and their characters I gain new perspective and fresh insight about myself and living a life of faith. Jesus used stories and parables to communicate the truth of the gospel. And we can find some of God's truth in fiction and literature. If we are alert to the movement of the Holy Spirit, God sometimes speaks to us through novels.

Curl Up with a Good Novel

Reading fiction is both a spiritual discipline and a cherished pleasure in my life. Some novels have even taught me more about experiencing the gospel and the kingdom of God than any theological text. The characters in novels can be companions through dark, anxious times, though they have never lived outside the pages of a novel.

There are no real steps to reading fiction with the eyes of faith. Simply choose a novel and begin to read, paying close attention to any insights God may give you. Following, I offer examples of three of my all-time favorite novels.

How I Did It

In *Busman's Honeymoon* by Dorothy Sayers, mystery writer Harriet Vane finally marries the dazzling Lord Peter Wimsey. I eagerly devoured the first six Lord Peter Wimsey mystery novels as the dashing, witty Lord Peter solved crime after crime. But it was the character Harriet Vane, in the final four books of the series, whom I came to love best.

Harriet Vane first makes her appearance in *Strong Poison*, where she is on trial for murder. Harriet, twenty-nine years old, is of rather plain appearance. She plays the role of a successful mystery writer, an independent woman who makes her own way in the world (and, coincidentally, shares the same name as I). Lord Peter falls in love with Harriet at first sight and vows to prove she is completely innocent of all wrong doing. The first time Lord Peter meets Harriet (in prison), he asks her to marry him, but she refuses. She even refuses his proposal after he proves she is innocent of murder and the court pronounces her "not guilty." And she continues to refuse marriage to Lord Peter through three more novels ("Certainly not" is Harriet's refrain). She refuses to marry him just because she is grateful to Lord Peter for saving her life. Harriet wants her marriage to be grounded on more than gratitude. As she continues to get involved in one sensational murder after another, Harriet refuses to use wealthy Lord Peter's offers of marriage as a way of escape or as a way to make life easier for herself. Before she consents to marry him (three novels and five years later), Harriet must find her own way through various trials and tribulations and so learn to value herself rather than find her value in the eyes of another human being, no matter how wonderful he is.

I discovered the Dorothy Sayers novels at a time in my life when I was seeking a way to escape. I had just moved to Los Angeles (not an easy city to get used to) and was working at a new and very demanding job. It was a dark time of high anxiety, wrenching transition, and dramatic change for me—spiritually and professionally. God seemed remote, and friends were few. I wanted God to rescue me from the new job I'd gotten myself into. I wanted God to return me to civilization—back home in San Francisco.

Though the novels were not Christian books, God showed me some things. The fictional Harriet had to learn to live through anxious times, refusing a convenient means of escape from trying situations. I learned that God doesn't always rescue single women from extremely anxious situations; instead, God was simply asking me to have faith in him and the gifts he'd given me.

The Dorothy Sayers' books also introduced me to the world of mystery. I enjoy reading mysteries for revelation. The best part of a mystery novel is when the mystery is finally revealed, the answer is given to the question "who-dun-it?", the moral of the story is well learned (crime doesn't pay), and justice and order are restored once again.

Reading mystery novels reminds me that there is an end to all things, a time when all things will be revealed and all wrongs will be put to rights. The characters of Lord Peter Wimsey and Harriet Vane show me that my spiritual pilgrimage has a destination to reach. Reading mysteries makes me wonder about that final revelation when, at the end of our pilgrimage, the thrill of the revelation of all things awaits us.

It has been said that all good fiction is good autobiography. Books written in the first person give the reader an opportunity to know the character (and often the author) in an especially intimate way. Such narratives are confessional. The main character speaks directly to us revealing his or her most hidden, deeply held feelings, thoughts, and motivations. As readers, we are allowed to peer into the very soul of another—an opportunity we are rarely permitted in real life. In doing so, we can gain a whole new perspective on the anxious situations in which we find ourselves.

For instance, God spoke to me through the classic novel, *To Kill a Mockingbird,* by Harper Lee. In the book, Margaret Finch reminiscences about one childhood summer in a small town in Alabama. As the story progresses, her father, Atticus Finch, comes to embody the essence of justice and mercy.

To Kill a Mockingbird is the story of three children and their fascination with a quiet, extremely shy man named Boo Radley who has shut himself up in his house next door. Throughout the summer the children try to entice Boo to come outside his house so they can see him. It is also the story of Tom Robinson, a black man unjustly accused, tried, and convicted for raping a white woman, Mayella Ewell. Atticus Finch is Tom's lawyer.

On presenting his son Jem with his first air rifle, Atticus said, "I know you'll go after birds. Shoot all the bluejays you want, if you can hit 'em, but remember it's a sin to kill a mockingbird." Atticus teaches his children (and us) how to live with the mockingbirds of this world—those innocents like Tom Robinson and Boo Radley who do no harm to anyone and whose simple human dignity makes beautiful music like the song of a mockingbird; and even trouble-makers like Bob and Mayella Ewell, victims of grinding poverty and unspeakable ignorance. Speaking to Scout (Margaret's childhood nickname), Atticus says, "First of all, if you can learn a simple trick, Scout, you'll get along a lot better with all kinds of folks. You never really understand a person until you consider things from his point of view . . . until you climb into his skin and walk around in it."

God, upon becoming human, climbed into our skin and walked around in it. Inside the human skin of Jesus, justice and mercy meet at last. And through the story of little Scout, I hear Christ's call to practice the gospel, to get out of my anxiety-ridden head for a little while and risk walking around in somebody else's skin so that I, too, may be an instrument of Christ's justice and mercy.

The grace of God will always feel to me like the story of *Jane Eyre* by Charlotte Brontë. *Jane Eyre* is of the classic love stories of nineteenth-century England. For me, *Jane Eyre* symbolizes the often stormy love story between God and his people. The story is a parable of the wildness of God's grace. The main character, Jane, grows up in an orphanage under appalling physical and emotional conditions. As a young woman, Jane is offered a way out of misery as she becomes governess to the widowed Mr. Rochester's only child. Rochester is a dark and moody man, but Jane nonetheless falls in love with him. Her faithfulness and love transform Rochester into an almost gentle man, and he asks Jane to marry him. At the altar, Jane learns of Mr. Rochester's dark secret and decides to leave him. During her absence, Rochester is blinded in a fire and spends many years a chastened man. Jane ultimately returns to Rochester and forgives him. Though the couple is reunited in the end, intense suffering has deepened and intensified their love.

Jane Eyre's turbulent relationship with Rochester reminds me that the grace of Christ often comes to us in the form of "servant love"—a love that grows and deepens in spite of overwhelming suffering and long absence from the beloved. It is no accident that Jane Eyre's last words are "Amen—even so come, Lord Jesus!" It is for love's sake that Jesus will not rest until he takes his church—broken, a little blind, but deeply loved—to himself.

I read my first science fiction novel—*Rocket to Alpha Centauri*—when I was eleven years old. It was a story about telepathic beings who lived in caves up high in cliffs on the planet Alpha Centauri. The overwhelming wonder I experienced when I first read that book has remained with me until this day. I went on to read the great masters of science fiction's golden age—Issac Asimov, Ray Bradbury, and Arthur C. Clarke. Long before I became a Christian, science fiction introduced me to the possibility of another reality not accessible to me through my senses. In a way, reading these books throughout my childhood and adolescence prepared me for a time many years in the future when I would hear and believe in the gospel.

The power of wonder and awe is important to Christian faith, especially for anxious people. Wonder has the power to take us out of ourselves for a time. When the Master returns, I am convinced that one of the great, overwhelming feelings humanity will experience is wonder. Great Christian writers like C.S. Lewis and J.R.R. Tolkien used science fiction and fantasy to inspire wonder and faith in readers. These writers knew the power of wonder to transform the lives of their characters—and their readers.

In Lewis's *Space Trilogy,* the character Ransome becomes a very different man by the third book, a man who has seen many wonders and is transformed by them. And in Tolkien's magnum opus, *The Lord of the Rings*, the hobbits return to the shire, transformed by wonders that inspired in them hidden courage and strength. Ray Bradbury's *Martian Chronicles* taught me that, like the Earth colonists on Mars, I, too, could choose to live in old destructive patterns, or I could surrender in wonder to the God whose ways are not my own.

Getting Started

Reading fiction can be a wonderful part of a regular time of study. But if reading fiction doesn't thrill you, nonfiction books can be read in a similar way. Getting started all by yourself, though, can be a little intimidating. It is easier to be held accountable for reading on a regular basis in the context of a small group. Many churches have found value and fun in forming literary small groups that meet together to read a novel or book and discuss what it means for Christian faith. Although the format varies, these groups usually consist of ten people or less who meet together once a month.

If you start a literary small group, decide how long the group sessions will be. (I find it difficult for everyone to have a chance to discuss a book in less than two hours.) It is helpful at the first meeting to make a list of books the group will be reading together over the next few months. A leader may be appointed to do a little research on the life (and faith, if applicable) of the author. The leader may then draw up a list of questions to guide the discussion of the book's author, characters, plot, and their implications for faith. For example, Why is this book important to me? Who is my favorite character? Why am I attracted to this character and what does that say about me and my faith? How am I like or unlike this character? What does this character tell me about God? Questions like these should be distributed to the members of the group before they begin to read the book.

The format and choice of books will vary greatly from

group to group. One group may choose to read only novels written by Christians. Another group may decide to read only women writers. Still another group may wish to vary its reading—an English classic one month, a mystery the next, a contemporary American work after that. Yet another group may want to alternate between Bible study and reading books.

If you're shy or you don't find small groups helpful, you can create your own questions and record your answers in a journal as you read. The wonderful part about writing down your thoughts and reflections is that you can also reflect on how the book affects your spiritual life.

The clock in the study strikes two in the morning. My eyes feel like sandpaper. I rub them until little points of color begin to swirl behind my closed eyelids. I open my eyes and look at my computer screen. *They're just words,* I say to myself. *All this work to make all these words.*

The words on the screen begin to form a circle. I blink hard and look again. The circle of words begins to spin, slowly at first and then faster and faster until the circle is one seamless, spinning band. Just as I am about to push the restart button on my computer to clear the screen, the word *grace* spins out of the circle, flies off the screen, and whizzes by my left ear, making a little "ping" sound as it passes. Then *mercy* flings from the screen and buzzes the top of my head. Faster and faster, all kinds of words begin to zing off the computer screen, darting around my head and shoulders. "Ping, ping, ping!" I dodge *joy*, duck *gentleness*; *peace* grazes my right cheek, *hope* brushes the back of my neck. Suddenly there is stillness and silence. The words hang in the air. The circle on the screen begins to form the Greek letter for Omega. I hear the Word softly say, "I am the Alpha and the Omega, the First and the Last."

Blessed are those who stay alert. The Spirit of God still moves over the face of the earth. The Master is at hand.

CHAPTER 7

the Bathroom:
Repentance

[Jesus] said to his disciples, "Therefore I tell you, do not worry about your life, what you will eat, or about your body, what you will wear. For life is more than food, and the body more than clothing. Consider the ravens: they neither sow nor reap, they have neither storehouse nor barn, and yet God feeds them. Of how much more value are you than the birds! And can any of you by worrying add a single hour to your span of life? If then you are not able to do so small a thing as that, why do you worry about the rest?" Luke 12:22–26

It's 5:30 Monday morning. The alarm buzzes. Yanked out of a deep sleep, I wonder who I am for a minute. Then I remember, "Oh, yeah. I'm Harriet . . . something." I shut off the alarm and stagger into the bathroom, where I turn on the light and try to make my eyes work. Then comes the moment of truth. I lean over the sink and look into the bathroom mirror. Bathroom mirrors don't lie. The image staring back at me is a forty-year-old woman with graying brown hair, standing up in tufts and hanging tangled over her face. Crow's feet are etched deeply into the corner of the only visible eye squinting through the tangles. Her brow shows a lifetime of worry. Her face is mottled by old freckles erratically covering a pasty complexion; her mouth sags and her chin and jowls are sinking south. "Oh, God!" I whisper through sleep-thick lips.

And in between me and the mirror is a simple wooden cross. How valuable I am! And can I by worrying add a single hour to my life? If then I am not able to do so small a thing as that, why do I worry?

My bathroom is small. The walls and window trim are painted a bright white. The original 1928 hexagon tile decorates the floor with a small cornflower blue design on a white field. The bathtub is big and deep; it is also original to the house. The tile work surrounding the tub enclosure is white with a cornflower blue row of tile at eye level. The toilet is also original and is of the same not-bright-white-but-not-off-white porcelain color as the tub. In between the tub and the toilet is a wall with a large window covered with blue mini-blinds. A 1920s reproduction pedestal sink sits next to the toilet. Next to the sink is a large linen closet where I keep towels, cosmetics, toiletries, and cleaning supplies. The bathroom is decorated with pale yellow towels, shower curtain, and area rug. On one wall hangs a large hand-painted tile picturing a big, smiling sunshine in a blue sky.

The bathroom is the place for cleansing. We visit the bathroom several times a day to cleanse ourselves of waste and dirt. It is in the bathroom that we daily confront our mortality. We are human beings who age and eventually die. Oh sure, after a long shower or a hot soak in the tub we may feel refreshed and relaxed. Yet a glance in the bathroom mirror tells us we are only flesh and blood after all—not the immortal gods we secretly believed ourselves to be in our youth. But consider the ravens. Of how much more value are we than the birds!

Not long ago my father was cleaning out his attic when he found my 1963 Barbie doll with an auburn, bubble hairdo. He also found four boxes of Barbie clothes, as well as Ken, Midge, Allan, Skipper, and Scooter. My mother called to tell me that Dad found Barbie and friends, and asked whether they should donate them to the Goodwill. I remember yelling into the phone, "No! Please don't! I haven't seen Barbie in twenty-eight years."

My parents brought Barbie, her friends, and all those clothes over to my house the following weekend. Ignoring Midge, Ken, and the rest of them, I opened the black patent-leather Barbie fashion case that housed my Barbie all those years. I found the "teenage fashion model" looking just as she did when a twelve-year-old Harriet retired Barbie so long ago. Her hair was perfect. Her fingers and toes still had the factory-original red fingernail polish on them. Her arms and legs worked perfectly. Her half-lidded eyes still had the blue eye shadow of the sixties; her lips were red and formed in the famous Barbie pout. Barbie was perfect. Except for the five o'clock shadow. Of a greenish hue, it covered Barbie's cheeks and chin from ear to ear. Twenty-eight years ago, I forgot to remove Barbie's earrings, which had copper in them. The copper had slowly leeched out of the earrings over the years to give Barbie a sick-looking beard.

At first I was very disappointed over Barbie's beard. (My other dolls were perfectly preserved.) I dressed Barbie in her bathing suit, treated her face with lemon juice, and set her out in the sunshine. When that didn't work, I tried rubbing alcohol, then bleach—then a solution of trisodium phosphate, but to no avail. Finally, I called a friend of mine who is a chemist, and he told me the only thing that would work was hydrochloric acid. Shocked, I asked, "Won't that take off half her face?" "Quite possibly," he answered.

So now Barbie lives in a retirement home for teenage fashion models—on a shelf in my study. Though she still dresses elegantly, she always wears sunglasses and a hat to help hide her deformity. Barbie's friends are flawlessly preserved; they live in a box in the closet.

Barbie was my all-time favorite, the best doll I ever had. I was nine years old when Barbie was given to me as a Christmas present. We went everywhere together. I took Barbie to school. Summers were spent playing Barbie with the other girls in the neighborhood. Not only did I love Barbie, I grew up thinking I was going to look just like her, have lots of clothes, and live in a dream house. Thirty-one years later, the bathroom mirror shows me a face with mortality's five o'clock shadow etched on it. And now I know that God doesn't make dolls—he makes human beings.

An old man dressed in a dirty white robe wanders through the corridors of San Francisco's financial district. To let him pass, a sea of investment bankers, traders, and stock brokers part before him like waves before a tanker. The old man's gray hair and beard are long and matted. Over his shoulder he carries a large sign on which is painted crudely, "Repent! The end is near!" As he shuffles along, he occasionally shouts, "Sinners!" and mumbles something about "perish" and "hellfire" and "damnation." His eyes are open very wide. Do his eyes behold prophetic vision, or the terrors of dementia?

For better or worse, this is popular culture's view of "repentance." Ask the proverbial man-on-the-street to describe repentance, and he'll most likely tell you it involves feeling guilty, worthless, sorry, and depressed. When I was looking for inspiration to write about repentance, I asked my computer's thesaurus to suggest other words for *repent*. What I got was:

> grieve, mourn, weep, bemoan, lament,
> regret, bewail, sorrow

My favorite is *bewail*. Bewail makes me imagine myself dressed in a Victorian gown as I fling myself to the drawing room floor, with great weeping and gnashing of teeth, where I pound my fists on the Persian carpet and curse the day I was born.

Anxiety much prefers a sackcloth-and-ashes approach to repentance rather than simply bathing in the light of Jesus' grace. It whispers, "Better to take control of your salvation and go find some ashes." Anxiety would have us bewail our humanity, flog ourselves into submission, march us in lockstep all the way to the gates of heaven, and present us for inspection—which, of course, we will fail because we are a worthless lot. This is the stuff of slavery.

The beginning of repentance is an honest admission to God of sin. Being honest to God about sin will trigger feelings of regret, remorse, even shame. And it should because we know we are capable of being so much more in the name of Christ. When we repent we experience *honest* regret, remorse, and shame. And then there is the anxious, nervous, dishonest exaggeration of those feelings—feelings of worthlessness, fear, and lingering guilt—because, bottom line, we don't trust in the cross of Christ which makes us more valuable to God than all the angels.

The English word *repent* tells only part of the story. The New Testament Greek word for repent means to stop traveling in one direction and turn 180 degrees around. While this New Testament word also communicates that one should feel sorrow and regret for his or her sin, the stress is on turning around and traveling back. Repentance is returning to God in whose likeness we are created.

Repentance is homecoming. To repent is to stop traveling away from God and to return to be cleansed in the grace and mercy of Jesus Christ. But we don't return home empty-handed. We bring God the gift of our humanity, which bears Christ's image. God loves us because we are human beings created in his image. God hates sin because it dehumanizes us; sin makes slaves out of heirs to God's kingdom, just as the prodigal son slaved away in a pig pen.

To repent is to begin the journey homeward again. Often we make that journey daily, bearing our humanity cleansed by Christ's grace. And our Father sees us from afar off, not as something to be despised, but something to be redeemed.

While God loves us because we are human, the world despises our humanity. Our culture bombards us with the message that simply being human is simply not enough. Advertising constantly tells us we are not beautiful enough, not sexy enough, not healthy enough, not clean enough, not happy enough, not young enough, not successful enough, not powerful enough, not well-dressed enough, and not well-fed enough. At school or on the job many of us learn we're not good enough. Too often in church we're told that we're not doing (or giving) enough. The result is anxiety, which feeds on the fear that it's too late and there will never be enough. "Do not worry about your life, what you will eat, or about your body, what you will wear. For life is more than food and the body more than clothing" (Luke 12:22).

Worst of all, our culture tells us we are not valuable enough. In spite of all the rhetoric about the value of the individual, we live in a country where human life is cheap. More children die from child abuse and neglect than any childhood disease. Guns kill more teenagers than any other cause of death today. A heat wave in Chicago kills forty-one elderly people who are buried *en masse* in a potter's grave, because no one comes to claim their bodies. There were *only* fifty-two murders in Oakland last year. A prisoner on parole from a murder sentence brutally beats and rapes a woman for five hours in a quiet upstate New York town. About three hundred people die of AIDS every day. Drunk drivers slaughter thousands every year. In our world, human beings are dehumanized by the numbers. But Jesus calls each one by name. "Of how much more value are you than the birds!"

What in the world does God see in us anyway? He sees human beings. He sees the cross. He sees Jesus. Like Jesus, we die. Like Jesus, we live again. We may be a little lower than the angels now, but we are created for a higher realm. We are Christ-bearers—redeemed and royal heirs to the kingdom. "Do not worry. . . ."

To Save a Wretch Like Me

Now all the tax collectors and sinners were coming near to listen to him. And the Pharisees and the scribes were grumbling and saying, "This fellow welcomes sinners and eats with them." So he told them this parable:

"What woman having ten silver coins, if she loses one of them, does not light a lamp, sweep the house, and search carefully until she finds it? When she has found it, she calls together her friends and neighbors, saying, 'Rejoice with me, for I have found the coin that I had lost.' Just so, I tell you, there is joy in the presence of the angels of God over one sinner who repents."

Luke 15:1–3, 8–10

Ever since we were thrown out of Eden, our survival has been at stake. We worry about how to provide for ourselves and our families, how to protect ourselves from the elements and from crime (before Eden was even a memory, Cain slew Abel). Anxiety results when we believe our survival or the survival of loved ones are threatened. Will my marriage survive? Can I survive another day in that office? Will this neighborhood survive? Will I have enough money to survive in old age? Will my kids survive me? Will I survive my kids?

It is so easy to get lost in anxiety. With fretting and worrying and vain imaginings we wander further and further from our heart's true home. We believe the lie that somehow we are in control of our lives and that somehow doing more or being better will fix everything. But there comes a day when, by the grace of God, we finally see that anxiety changes nothing, that no amount of worrying or dreaming up endless scenarios about the future can change even one, tiny, little thing. We feel so far away and wonder how we got there, how it all got to be so crazy. And we want to go home. Then we turn around to find that we were already found. "Amazing grace! I once was lost, but now am found."

Like the woman who overturns the cushions and sweeps the floors to find one lost coin, God moves heaven and hell to find one sinner who repents. In finding us, God saves us. God doesn't rescue us. God doesn't remove us from sinning or from everything and anyone that causes us anxiety. Rather than have our worries magically disappear or all temptation to sin vanish, God liberates us from the very *power* of sin that dehumanizes us and makes us slaves. God saves us. He washes away the power of sin and anxiety to reveal the dignity and glory of our humanity—beings made in the likeness of God. Sin itself remains; worrisome people and situations remain. But God destroys their power to rob us of God himself.

A Final Word

"Which one of you, having a hundred sheep and losing one of them, does not leave the ninety-nine in the wilderness and go after the one that is lost until he finds it? When he has found it, he lays it on his shoulders and rejoices. And when he comes home, he calls together his friends and neighbors, saying to them, 'Rejoice with me, for I have found my sheep that was lost.' Just so, I tell you, there will be more joy in heaven over one sinner who repents than over ninety-nine righteous persons who need no repentance.

Luke 15:4–7

The old man wandering the streets of San Francisco was right to identify us as sinners, but he was wrong to call for repentance by using threats. We are not frightened into the kingdom; we are *loved* into the kingdom. Repentance is an opportunity for joy.

My conversion to Christianity at twenty-two years of age was pretty dull. I didn't have a drug or alcohol problem; I wasn't involved in a destructive relationship; I was not physically disadvantaged; I did not play sports. I was, however, a student teacher.

Family and friends had told me all through high school and college that I'd be a fine teacher (although I didn't major in education in college). I believed them. Immediately after graduating from college, I enrolled in a secondary education teacher training program to learn how to teach social studies and government to junior high and high school students. My first student teaching assignment was teaching social studies at an inner-city junior high school. After unsuccessfully trying to break up a fist fight in class between two fourteen-year-olds who were bigger and taller than me, I knew that teaching was probably not the career for me.

Suddenly I had no career plans. The future lay before me dark and forbidding. Anxiety drove me into a frenzy. I had a dear college friend, Laura, who happened to be a Christian. She and I passionately debated the Bible, the gospel, Jesus, and religion throughout our years together in school. Mostly, Laura was simply my friend. She listened to me rant and rave, and every now and then she told me how much Jesus loved me. Because Laura loved me, I came to believe Jesus loved me too. I repented of my obsessive need to control my future (not for the last time) and joyfully fell into Jesus' arms.

Joy is the serious business of heaven. "There will be more joy in heaven over one sinner who repents than over ninety-nine righteous persons who need no repentance." Jesus Christ has the last word. Not death. Not sin. Not anxiety. Not fear. The last word is joy. "Rejoice with me, for I have found my sheep that was lost."

There is no repentance without the grace of Jesus Christ. Grace pursues us, finds us, and taps us on the shoulder. And when we turn around, Jesus stands beside us, with arms wide open in welcome. Repentance is the joyful acceptance of the grace of Jesus Christ.

A friend once explained to me how grace works. "You remember the old Sears and Montgomery Ward department stores?" he asked. "Somewhere in each store there was a vacuum blowing air through its nozzle. On the column of air was a spinning beach ball. Grace is like that column of air. We may not see it or feel it, but the grace of God literally sustains us." The grace of God calls us to repentance. We may, by grace, turn around, but it is God alone who carries us home.

Repentance involves confession—not just confession of sin, but confession of faith. "Jesus is Lord" is the earliest confession of the Christian church. In the early church, a candidate for baptism had to turn away from sin and Satan. In the baptismal ceremony the candidate physically turned around to face the opposite direction. But that was only half of repentance. The candidate also had to confess his or her faith and declare to the congregation that Jesus is Lord.

My most deeply rooted abiding sin is the need to be in control, which, like a Pandora's box, continually releases the demons of anxiety, worry, vain imaginings, and ineffectual striving. I'm no different from other anxious people. Lurking somewhere behind all anxiety is our need to control an uncertain, threatening situation or person. The survival of the early church was threatened by persecution from outside and various heresies from within. Those early Christians rooted their faith in a simple confession. For anxious people in the twentieth century, it all boils down to the same confession— "Jesus is Lord."

Is this a magic formula to make us feel better and remove all threat and anxiety? No. When we confess "Jesus is Lord," we turn from the sin of trying to be in control. When we confess "Jesus is Lord," we are bathed and cleansed in the limitless mercy and grace of God.

I was so exhausted I could hardly take another step. My face was smudged with dirt, and my old clothes were covered in dust and cobwebs from following the contractor through the crawl space under the house. *How can I feel so far from home without ever leaving the house?* I think sadly.

I had just learned that the house was in an earthquake test zone on the Hayward Fault. The contractor told me to bolt the house to its foundation and reinforce the brick chimney. Where would the money come from? Even if I found the money to strengthen my home for an earthquake, there were no guarantees of survival. The Big One was coming any minute now—one that would register 8.0 or greater on the Richter scale. The ground would just open under the house and swallow it up. There would be nothing left but splinters and a big, dark, jagged tear in the earth where my home used to be.

I stand at the very center of the kitchen, tears spilling from my eyes and making tracks on my dirty cheeks. Try as I might, I simply wouldn't be able to keep the earth from moving. All the investment, all the hard work, all the worry and endless anxious nights—all for nothing. There was nothing I could do, nowhere to go, no one to turn to. "Jesus is Lord," I whisper, hardly believing it, as I wipe my eyes with the back of a filthy hand.

As I turn to take a shower, an intense light streams through the bathroom door. Startled, I can barely see through my tears and the bright light. Half blind from squinting, I feel someone push me hard from behind, and I stumble through the door and into the middle of the light. A wind begins to swirl around me, faster and faster. The shower curtain flies away, the towels are whipped from their racks. A scent of pure lavender fills the room.

Terrified, but exhilarated too, I watch as the tub and sink each fill with warm water and overflow onto the tile floor. The water is ankle deep and rising. There is absolutely nothing I can do. Helpless, I sit down on the floor in the middle of the rising water. And someone begins to laugh. I'm startled at first, but the laughter keeps echoing around the room. I begin to laugh too. Laughing, I splash my face with water. Looking up, I see Jesus, his arms open wide. His eyes are smiling. And I know I am home once again.

Endnotes

Chapter 1

1. Annie Dillard, *Pilgrim at Tinker Creek* (New York: Harper & Row, 1974).
2. C.S. Lewis, *The Lion, the Witch, and the Wardrobe* (New York: HarperCollins, 1978).

Chapter 3

1. Anne Lamott, *Operating Instructions: A Journal of My Son's First Year* (New York: Fawcett, 1993).

Chapter 4

1. Sayers, Dorothy, *The Mind of the Maker* (San Francisco: Harper San Francisco, 1987).
2. "Calling Cards," *Victoria*, Aug. 1995, 25.
3. Anne Lamott, *Bird by Bird: Some Instructions on Writing and Life* (New York: Pantheon, 1994).

Chapter 5

1. Carol Lee Flinders, *Enduring Grace: Living Portraits of Seven Women Mystics* (New York: HarperCollins, 1993).
2. Ibid.
3. Julian of Norwich, *A Book of Showings to the Anchoress Julian of Norwich,* 1993.
4. Julian of Norwich, *Revelations of Divine Love*, 1982.

5. Esther de Waal, *Living with Contradiction* (New York: Harper & Row, 1989).

Chapter 6

1. Macrina Wiederkehr, *A Tree Full of Angels: Seeing the Holy in the Ordinary* (New York: Harper & Row, 1988).
2. Ibid.